Introduction

Are you like me? Do you experience a slight frisson of excitement when you spot amber warning beacons up ahead on the motorway, a sure sign that you are going to pass a '*convoi exceptionnel*'? Tank transporters, excavators, chemical vessels, bridge sections, railway locomotives... the bigger the better as far as I'm concerned.

These days, any load too large or too heavy for conventional road-going trucks and trailers requires permission from the Highways Agency to use the UK's roads. The *Road vehicles (authorisation of special types) (general) order 2003* – generally abbreviated to STGO – regulates the operation of trucks and trailers which do not comply with the normal provisions of the *Road traffic act 1988*. STGO divides abnormal loads into three categories: 50,000kg, 80,000kg and 150,000kg and it is the last category – 'STGO CAT 3' – that covers the real monsters.

In the 1950s and '60s, things weren't quite so well regulated. Special permission was still needed to move a heavy load but the drivers and operators were a real breed apart. They frequently designed their own trucks and trailers, they knew everything that there was to know about lifting and moving heavy loads, and they performed feats that the ordinary driver might have thought impossible.

Back then, in the days before motorways criss-crossed the country, you might have found yourself standing on an over-bridge watching a pair of Wynns' Pacifics or Diamond Ts, resplendent in the company's glossy red and black livery, hauling a 100-ton transformer up a steep incline, or watching the crew inch it round an impossibly tight bend with ancient buildings on either side. Or perhaps a pair of Scammell Contractors, one pushing, one pulling, struggling with a huge fractionating column across an uneven dock apron.

Now consider the problems involved in shifting tanks.

Years ago I used to travel the A303 and it wasn't uncommon to catch sight of a convoy of Scammell tank transporters, each with its Challenger tank load. These days it is more likely to be the British Army's Oshkosh M1070... a truck the size of a small apartment block!

But even though the loads are smaller these days and the trucks perhaps lack the magic of the good old days there are still some sights to be seen. The other day I passed a five-axle Faun tractor on the M25 belonging to ALE... it was struggling up the rise from the Dartford Bridge to the A2 with an enormous excavator. It was a fine sight but I couldn't help thinking back to the good old days when an abnormal load really *was* abnormal.

So, if like me you enjoy the sights and sounds of today's heavy haulage then I know you'll enjoy reliving the memories of yesteryear. In these pages you'll find a feast of monster trucks – Scammells, Antars, Pacifics, Diamond Ts, the elusive Rotinoff and a brace of lesser-known foreigners. All of them devoted to shifting those exceptional loads.

Pat Ware

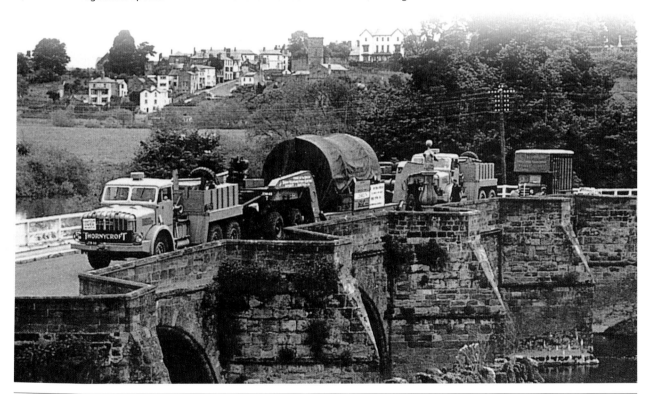

Published by
KELSEY PUBLISHING LTD
Printed by William Gibbons Ltd on behalf of
Kelsey Publishing Ltd, Cudham Tithe Barn, Berry's Hill, Cudham, Kent TN16 3AG
Tel: 01959 541444 *Fax:* 01959 541400 *Email:* kelseybooks@kelsey.co.uk *Website:* www.kelsey.co.uk
©2008 **ISBN: 978-1-873098-89-9**

Contents

6   Pacific Result

12   Mighty Antar!

17   Truck stop: Scammell Pioneer

Who Dares Wynns:

18   *Part 1:* Origins

23   Truck stop: Pacific TR1

24   *Part 2:* The Diamond and Pacific years

30   *Part 3:* Old soldiers never die

36   *Part 4:* The challenges of nationalisation

42   *Part 5:* Powerful contractions

48   *Part 6:* Export or die!

53   *Part 7:* 'In the Deserts of Sudan'

57   *Part 8:* Still in Sudan

61   *Part 9:* On the road again

66   Antar Eater?
68   The Brontosaurus
70   Moving the tanks
76   Volat
78   HET-70
80   Scammell Contractor tank transporter
83   War is an ugly thing
87   Here be dragons
91   Truck stop: Oshkosh M1070F
92   Commander
98   Snowy Mountain Antars
100 Pacification!
104 Counting chickens
108 Diamonds and rust
116 Antar, poet warrior
120 Thornycroft Antar Mk2
126 Antars again

PACIFIC RESULT

(Photos: Nick Larkin)

Thirty years after leaving service with legendary heavy haulage contractor Wynns, this extraordinary Pacific has been unveiled after major restoration. Nick Larkin reports.

Unveiled in all its glory – Mike Lawrence's former Wynns Pacific

Roller shutter doors slide open to reveal...

....Pacific... finally edging out into the sunshine....

... roaring on to rally at Highbridge event....

John Wynn back in the Pacific's cab after 30 years - and feeling very much at home.

Much repanelling carried out to the rear of the vehicle.

No wonder there was so much anticipation in the air - as if we were awaiting a royal visitor or even a *Coronation Street* celebrity. Everyone was looking forward to seeing for real a star most had only previously admired in black and white photos.

Finally the time had arrived.

We heard her before they opened the roller shutter doors - and she sounded like thunder. Finally, the door rose to reveal ... the ex-Wynns Pacific, Enterprise, in all its huge gleaming red glory.

On to the rally field she roared, the clicking of cameras drowned by the supercharged Cummins engine. Finally, the Pacific was parked, ready to be besieged by admirers.

It was an event of raw emotion for many, not least former operator John Wynn, who hadn't sat in the cab for 30 years. "I well remember driving this vehicle and feel so at home in here, though I can't believe this Pacific has finally been restored. It looks wonderful," he said.

The day was also a milestone for present owner Mike Lawrence, who'd bought the beast in a sorry state 21 years earlier. The unveiling appropriately took place at Mike's Vintage Hay and Harvest event on his Somerset farm, an event raising £600 for the National Blind Children Society.

As well as being renowned as a tractor and lorry collector/restorer, Mike was for many years a major name in the low loader business.

Many people had helped with the complex restoration of the Pacific, which dwarfed tractors, lorries, people - in fact everything at the event.

Just like the restoration, it's difficult to know where to start with the story of this incredible vehicle. We really have to go back to 1943 in fact, when the first Pacific M6, or 'Dragon Wagon', appeared with the American Military.

The 6x6 armour-plated tractor had developed because of a dissatisfaction with the Diamond T's off-road capability, caused by the lack of a driven front axle.

The vehicle was designed by Knuckey Truck Company, San Francisco, a small firm best known for its mining and quarry trucks. Sadly, it didn't have the capacity for large scale production, so the contract was given to the Pacific Car and Foundry Company, of Renton, Washington. The semi-trailers were made by Freuhauf.

Overall weight of the tractor was 20.5 tons, and 37.6 tons with the trailer. And that was without a tank on board! In 1944, a non-armour-plated version arrived at a mere 12.32 tons.

A respectable 1272 examples were built, but only one was ever known to serve with British forces. Many Pacifics were used in heavy haulage after the war years but none

Above and Below: Pacific in its service days.

(Photos courtesy Mike Lawrence)

...and grabbing everyone's attention!

The Glory Days of Heavy Haulage

Down at heel Pacific at owner Mike Lawrence's yard.

Rear of cab needed rebuilding.

Cab repanelled and roof timbers, which had suffered due to water seeping in via panel pins were renewed. Seen here are Mike's partner, Pam and her sister, Rita.

Removal of ballast boxes revealed sound chassis but major cleaning being needed.

Repanelled and red oxided ballast boxes being replaced.

(All restoration photos: Mike Lawrence)

New exhaust made up.

Like all its sister vehicles, Wynns gave this Pacific a name.

were more famous than the fleet bought by Wynns.

HP Wynn heard of two dozen of the vehicles in a Kent quarry and six were bought for use, and a further four for spares.

Recalls John Wynn: "I can remember we paid about £400 each for them - a fraction of the cost of a new Scammell.

"After stripping off all the armour plating - there was about eight tons of that - which we sold at a good profit, obviously - the cabs were built by ourselves.

"Although they looked the same, there were never any measurements - they were all done on the floor and our carpenters did a wonderful job."

The rebuilds took place over a 14-year period as the vehicles were needed, the first appearing in September 1950 and the last, the star of this feature making its debut in December 1964.

John thought up names for all the vehicles - Dreadnought, Helpmate,

Conqueror. Challenger and Enterprise, which was registered ADW 228B. The only difference between the vehicles is that two (including Enterprise) had a back bogie 9ft 6in wide, against 11ft wide on the other four.

The Pacifics came with 240hp, 17.85 litre Hall-Scott petrol engines. "They were good engines, and had wonderful pulling power, but they'd only do about three gallons to the mile." said John.

The Pacifics ended up with Roots turbocharged Cummins 320 engines, bought reconditioned from Blackwood Hodge, Northampton, who were Terex and Euclid main dealers. The unit in Enterprise is believed to have originally been in a 1950s Euclid.

An eight-speed Self-Changing Gears gearbox was fitted.

Enterprise was withdrawn in 1973, and eventually landed up Sullivan's yard at Bedhampton, where Mike Lawrence became rather a fan of the machine.

"I used to visit from time to time.

Pacific retained its original six-wheel configuration from when it was a gun tractor.

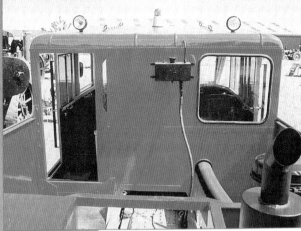

Pacific shows off newly rebuilt rear of cab.

I've always liked big vehicles. The Pacific stood there and I can remember looking up at it thinking: 'That's a great ugly thing…'"

Adds Mike: "I remember asking Mr Sullivan what he wanted for it and the amount was too much money for a bit of a plaything. He also had a very early low-loader trailer that had belonged to Norman Box and both were on offer when an auction was held. I went with an open mind, and ended up with the Pacific."

That was in 1982, and it would be a further seven years before efforts were made to start the engine. Mike recalls: "When I bought it I didn't think a lot about it at the time. John Wynn wrote a piece in Truck and Driver magazine in 1988 and said there was a Pacific (this one!) crying out for restoration. I remember thinking I must do something about it."

"The Pacific stood in our yard and to be honest, the condition hadn't been good when we got it, but it got worse. Eventually various jobs such as a gearbox rebuild were carried out and other things were done when there were people who could turn their hand to them. My son Ross starting doing bits when he was 10 or 11.

"Once the engine was started a nasty crack in the block was discovered, which luckily could be repaired with chemical metal.

"Other tasks were completed over the years, but it wasn't until last October that the final thrust began. "Several of us were having a cup of tea one Sunday afternoon and got on to the subject of the Pacific. People wanted to start there and then but I thought it was too late at 4pm, Next thing, the Pacific had been pushed into the workshop with a tractor and we never looked back."

First job was to tackle the ballast boxes on the back of the Pacific.

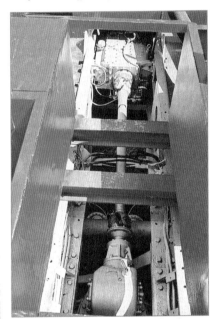

Now this is what you call heavy duty!

Fascinating centre pivot chain drive to the rear bogie was thankfully not in need of too much work.

Not a lot of space for the driver considering vehicle's size - instruments basically those available to Wynns in 1963.

(Photos Nick Larkin)

Mike Lawrence would like to thank everyone who helped and/or offered encouragement for this major project.

How they were - a sister Pacific in gun tractor guise.

(Photo courtesy John Wynn)

Most of the framework was okay but some pieces of the framework needed doing, new steel panels being fitted as needed.

Lifting off the ballast box framework to get at the chassis revealed a nasty surprise. The Pacific has a chain drive to the rear wheels and these are lubricated by a drip feed oiler.

Said Mike: "Over the years the oil had dried so hard we had to use an air chisel to get some of it off. Nothing else would touch it. We took the hubs and wheels off on one side. Just to clean the rear axle, the hubs and the chassis from the gearbox took 14-15 hours of steam cleaning - and that was a steam cleaner with a very short nozzle on it!"

Thankfully the chains of the chain drive were generally in good condition, apart from one needing some new sections making up. Interestingly, there are no springs on the back of the vehicle as such, just shock absorbers. There are leaf springs at the front. The system had survived well.

Next it was time to give the cab some attention, with attention being needed to framing at the rear. Then came a none too pleasant discovery, as Mike recalls: 'Timbers in the roof looked perfectly good, but the aluminium cladding had been put on with small panel pins. The wet had sort of followed these in and rotted the wood."

All this had to be replaced, Ron Skinner carrying out the work. The back of the cab was reskinned in aluminium and the roof resealed. Other panels were replaced as necessary.

All the mudguards had to be made from what was left of the originals as a pattern. Two in One Ducting of Cheddar doing an excellent job here.

The inside of the cab was etch primed, given two coats of undercoat and repainted.

Mike said: "The cab had been equipped with the instruments Wynns could buy in 1963 and some of these were replaced as necessary. Replacement indicators and lights were picked up at *CVC's* Donington show and windscreen motors and arms from the Great Dorset Steam Fair."

Now to the painting. The chassis was painted with red oxide and then sprayed with Tractol paint in Massey Ferguson Silver Mist. "Because the Pacific is so big, you're just using tin after tin after tin of paint," Mike recalls.

The cab was rubbed down to bare metal, etch primed, then five coats of Hi-Build red oxide primer were applied, followed by five coats of Post Office Red top coat.

Signwriting was entrusted to Graham Booth, who owns two Wynns Scammells, and did a great job.

The list of mechanical tasks included doing something about the compressor, which was cracked with frost damage. This was eventually replaced with one from a Cummins-powered ERF.

The clutch on the engine appeared to be the original - an American Lipe unit - and this was repaired.

The brakes were stripped and overhauled with Westinghouse cylinders and new rollers. No point on trying to do anything about the front brakes - there aren't any.

The axles were drained and fluid replaced, and the starter motor was replaced. The supercharger was in good working order.

New tyres were fitted on the front, costing £220 each from Kings Road Tyres of Ilminster - Mike had been quoted £300 from one firm in the 1980s.

Nothing wrong with the tyres or the fitting, but then, Mike recalls, disaster!

"We took the wheels down there shotblasted and brought them back painted. I loaded them into the back of my pick-up, which I left outside my workshop overnight. The pick-up was stolen and the wheels had gone as well. The pick-up was later found abandoned in a field - but the wheels weren't there. We spent a lot of time and had an appeal on local radio.

"A week later a man who works for a plant hire firm stopped in a lay-by and saw what he thought were pipe rims. They were, thankfully, the Pacific's wheels."

Finally, and with Mike's event looming, the Pacific was ready to show, The show (see news) was very much a Wynns reunion, with several vehicles present.

"We'd been building up to this for a long time and when we actually drove it out I must admit I was quite emotional. All those years I'd kept on thinking we must do it and finally we had.

"There's actually still some work to do to the electrics and ballast box floor so we won't be rallying the Pacific this year. Next year we hope to take it to events. After all this, we want to have some fun with this vehicle - we want a lot of people to enjoy seeing it. That would definitely give us pleasure."

The Glory Days of Heavy Haulage

(Photo courtesy John Wynn)

Pacific trio - vehicles were converted by Wynns as needed over a period of almost 15 years.

MIGHTY A

WIDE ROAD

Now this IS a heavy commercial. Alan Barnes tells the story of Thornycroft's massive Antar, with the help of Antar-owner Mervyn Annetts, a former apprentice at the factory.

Main photos: ALAN BARNES

As a young apprentice working for Thornycroft, Mervyn Annetts used to fit wheel nuts to brand new examples of the mighty and now legendary Antar.

He recalls: "Imagine a lad carefully working away, daydreaming of actually owning one of these monsters." Now he does!

Mervyn's Thornycroft career began in 1959, in what he calls "The hurly burly world of the company's cost office".

He says, "Although I started as an office boy, the training programme saw me move into the works where I spent

about six months in each of the various departments. At that time the company was producing models like the Trusty, Trident and Swiftsures, but the really big boys were the Antar and the Big Ben tractors."

Mervyn's other dream was to run a Bedford coach and this was realised when he bought an OB, registered HOD 75, in 1978. The vehicle is still in use today as part of the small fleet of coaches which Mervyn operates from his yard near Micheldever, Hants, working on school contracts and private hire.

It was 1995 when Mervyn realised his other transport dream when he bought

a 1954 Antar Mk 2 from Tony Potton. "This was great fun and I took it to rallies for many years, rattling along the road at 20 miles an hour and getting 2 miles to the gallon out of her. I never thought for a moment that I would ever part with her."

However, in 2005 Mervyn decided to sell the Mk 2 to Phil Rye, who was going to arrange for it to be exported to Australia. Phil's interest in the Antar stemmed from a wish to establish a museum dealing with the transport involved in the construction work of the Snowy Mountain hydro-electricity project in New South Wales.

Three Antars had been used on the

NTAR!

The Antar road train crossing the Murray River at Bringenbrong with equipment for the Murray Two power station in 1965.

Hauling a transformer from Island Bend to the Snowy Adit sub-station in 1961.

Antar 76224 transporting equipment from Cudgewa railhead to Murray Two power station at Khancoban in 1965.

NVS 131

You wouldn't want to get in the way of Mervyn Annetts' mighty Antar Mk 3. (Main photos: Alan Barnes)

Antars delivering equipment to Tumut Three power station, Talbingo, about 1970.

project but had all been scrapped many years ago. Phil's intention was to return his newly-acquired Antar Mk2 to "Snowy Mountain" condition.

However Mervyn was unwilling to part with his vehicle until a suitable replacement had been obtained, and the deal was not finally concluded until he was able to buy an Antar Mk 3A from John Riley, in Stockport.

SOME HISTORY

Until the late 1940s, the largest truck produced by Thornycroft had been the 12-ton Amazon, but after an approach from George Wimpey and Son in 1949,

the company began to work on the design for a new heavy tractor.

Wimpey's requirements were for a fleet of powerful tractors to be used by the Iraq Petroleum Company in the building of a new pipeline across the desert and CE Burton, chief designer at Thornycroft, was put in charge of the development project.

Progress was rapid, to say the least. Initial discussions took place in February, Wimpeys placed an order for 35 tractors in April, the first chassis (53781) was assembled in November, and by December the first Antar was being road-tested. ▶

Records are unclear as to how many of this unusual Antar variant were actually built.

New Antar Mk 3s at the Thornycroft Works in Basingstoke.

Wynns Heavy Haulage road-testing the two Antar /Crane trailer combinations destined for use on the Snowy Mountain Project in Australia.

The Mk 3 was a fifth-wheel version of the Antar while the Mk 3A was a ballast tractor. However they could be converted to either form as required.

35 Antars were supplied to Iraq Petroleum Company for use in the building of a 560-mile pipeline from Kirkuk to Banias. The eight-wheel articulated Crane semi-trailers were specially designed and loads of 63 tons were typical.

Although maintenance conditions were primitive, the rugged Antars proved their worth. A total of 50 Rover engines had been supplied for use in the Antars and all but seven were rebuilt during their time in the oilfields.

Power for the new monster came from an 18-litre Rover Meteorite Mk 101 engine, an eight-cylinder 250bhp indirect-injection unit coupled to a four-speed constant mesh gearbox and three-speed auxiliary box which enabled the Antar to reach 30mph in about 90 seconds.

For work in the oilfields, a new 45-ton skeletal semi-trailer was designed by Crane, of Dereham. The official launch of the new heavy tractor was on February 22, 1950 in a demonstration at the Fighting Vehicle Research and Development test track at Bagshot Heath, Surrey.

The Antar was an impressive success and almost immediately the first tractor was shipped out to begin work on the pipeline. The rest of the 34 vehicles were

built during the next two years, the last being delivered on May 16, 1951.

The Antars performed impressively in the arduous desert conditions and orders for further vehicles came from other companies, including McAlpine and

> "I never thought for a moment that I would ever part with her"

Shell. Wynns tested two Antars for the Snowy Mountain project.

While the initial development had been for commercial use, the power of the Antar had not gone unnoticed by military observers at the initial demonstration. The War Office was looking to replace its fleet of Scammell and Diamond T

tractors and the Antar appeared to be capable of handling the 50-ton trailers for carrying the new Centurion tank.

With the Army's involvement, design changes and improvements were called for. The Ministry of Supply ordered 15 of the Mk 1 in 1951, all of which were fitted with the Meteorite Mk 204 petrol engine. This initial batch of vehicles was followed over the next few years by the Mk 2, Mk 3 and Mk 3A and the Antar was destined to remain in service with British Army tank and engineer regiments for more than 30 years.

Mervyn says, "During my time at Thornycroft, I was really impressed by the new Antar Mk 3 and often tried to wangle a 'second man' turn when they had to go on the road. Any Antar being taken out on the road had to have a movement order and an extra person in the cab, and

occasionally the apprentices were given the chance to accompany the driver.

"I well remember day trips from the Basingstoke works along to one of the many Army depots around Salisbury Plain. Some of the roads were quite narrow but nothing seemed to be prepared to argue with an oncoming Antar!"

MERVYN's Mk 3A

John Riley bought his Mk 3A from a scrapyard in 1988 and spent four years restoring it and then rallying it for a while. He even made a couple of visits to Thornycroft's home town of Basingstoke.

It was eventually laid up again in 2001, and had been a little bit neglected for a few years until Mervyn arranged to buy it in 2005. With that deal concluded Mervyn could complete the sale of

his Mk 2 to Phil and he drove this to Southampton, where it was loaded on a ship bound for Australia.

"I was accompanied on that last drive by my friend Chris Tree, who filmed the day's activities so that I would have something to remember the old girl with," he said.

Thornycroft Society records show that 580 Antars of all types were supplied to the Army between 1951 and 1963. Mervyn's Antar is a Mk 3A FV12006 ballast tractor, chassis number 63135, and the building of the vehicle was completed on March 14, 1963.

Registered for military use as 12 DM 60, it was powered by a Rolls-Royce C8SFL eight-cylinder diesel engine. It entered Army service in March 1963 and was moved the following May to Germany where it joined 23 Tank

Transport Squadron of the British Army of the Rhine.

The vehicle remained on the Continent for several years, moving to 17 Reserve Vehicle Depot in September 1969 and then to the Ordnance Depot in Antwerp.

In January 1971, the Antar was moved again, this time to 602 Transport Unit where she took part in Exercise Emblem. A refit was carried out by the Fazakerley Engineering Company, Liverpool, in 1979 and when this work was completed the vehicle returned to 602 Transport Unit in Germany, where it remained until retired from service in February 1986.

Eventually the Army replaced its Antars with the Scammell Commander, which entered service in 1984.

As a heavy haulage tractor, the Antar in all its guises was very successful and Thornycroft sold some 700 of them. ▶

The Army took about 600 of the total but the others were sold to companies throughout the world, with a choice of Cummins, Detroit, Caterpillar and Rolls-Royce engines as well as a Thornycroft 11.3-litre diesel.

Some interesting variants were produced. A smaller version was sold as the Big Ben, and the Sandmaster was a short wheelbase 4x2 tractor with huge rear wheels designed for desert conditions. Esso bought 12 Sandmasters for use in the oilfields in Libya.

For a vehicle which had been designed and developed in a matter of a few months, the Mighty Antar certainly made an impact in the world of heavy haulage. As well as helping to bring the Thornycroft name to the fore in terms of heavy tractors, the Antars provided the Army with heavy duty transport for more than 30 years.

WORKING ON THE MK3

Although Mervyn's "new" Antar had not been used for a while, it was still in pretty sound mechanical condition, although the steering needed overhaul. A new power steering ram was fitted and some of the air lines were replaced. Mervyn had help from two friends, John Bond and Peter Roberts.

"You can't really get spares easily but you can normally do something," said Mervyn.

The second axle needed new bearings, and these were made up by Henderson Bearings, Ringwood, Hants, and Norman Aish supplied the oil seals.

The Turner 20-ton winch was in good condition.

Rotten areas on the cab, on the doors and around the windscreen, were replaced with new metal. Once that was completed the tractor was for a new coat of Army green.

"I had the whole family working on that, rubbing her down and putting on two coats of acrylic paint. We didn't need any undercoat as the paint that was on wasn't too bad. I finished her just in time to take her to the Basingstoke Transport Festival," said Mervyn.

LIFE WITH AN ANTAR

So what is the Antar Mk III like to drive? Mervyn says, "You have to be careful because of the width, especially in built-up areas, though it has power steering and the lock isn't too bad." Top speed is about 30mph, but fuel consumption is a bit restrictive at 4mpg.

Looking on the bright side: "At least the Mk 3 is a diesel. The Mk 2 was petrol and only did 2mpg," said Mervyn. The Antar goes out regularly, and it has been to events such as the Brickworks Rally at Bursledon and the Max Café gathering at Pabworth.

Mervyn says, "I really do enjoy driving the Antar. I did my apprenticeship at Thornycroft and delivered them new, and they are just part of my life."

ANTAR Mk 3 SPECIFICATION

Year	1963
Length	30ft
Width	10ft 6in
MPG	4
Top speed	30mph.
Height	11ft
Engine	Rolls-Royce C8SFL eight-cylinder
Gearboxes	(two) Thornycroft
Weight	(without ballast) 24 tons (approx)

THANKS

Our thanks to Mervyn Annetts for telling the tale of his two Antars and to Chris Tree of the Thornycroft Society for allowing the use of photographs from the society archives. Mervyn would like to hear from anyone who has any pictures of 12 DM 60 on active service.

Truck stop

An early Scammell Pioneer chassis demonstrates the extraordinary articulation available from the perch-bar pivoted front axle, whilst overall chains on the walking gearcase rear axle provide plenty of traction in the toughest conditions. Powered by a Gardner 6LW diesel, the Pioneer was always a willing performer which could be loaded way beyond the manufacturer's rating.

PART ONE WHO

John Wynn and Pat Ware look at the origins and activities of the legendary heavy-haulage company Robert Wynn & Sons... and in particular at the fascinating life of John Wynn

Sentinel DG4 steam wagon (Wynns' fleet number 25, DW 6440). Constructed in flat-bed form in June 1928 (works number 7746) and subsequently converted to a tractor for use with an articulated semi-trailer by Sentinel themselves.

Robert Wynn & Sons can trace its origins back to 1863 when Thomas Wynn purchased a couple of horses and carts and established himself as a carrier in the region of Newport, South Wales. At the time, he can have had little idea of the significance of his action but, a century later, the name of Wynns was synonymous with expertise in moving abnormal and heavy indivisible loads and the company

had become market leaders in their field, their name renowned across the world.

Thomas Wynn, the founder of the company, had been born in Devon in 1821 and started work in the Exeter region as a contract cleaner of railway carriages, eventually moving to Newport where he was employed by the Great Western Railway Company. Realising that there was an unfulfilled demand for road haulage in the South Wales valleys, he offered his services for the onward

movement of the goods which were being carried to Newport by rail, and which up to that time had been distributed by canal or packhorse. Thomas also formed an alliance with the Newport-based Star Flour Mills, an arrangement which was to last the best part of a century, distributing flour to the bakeries in the valleys.

Thomas died in 1878, by which time the company had expanded to include several dozen horses and carts... those new-fangled horseless carriages had yet

DARES WYNNS!

Acquired in February 1942, this Foden 6x4 ballast tractor (Wynns' fleet number 112, DDW 18) served with the heavy-haulage side of the business throughout WW2. One of only three said to have been built, the vehicle was easily capable of hauling 100 tons. In one view, a 10-year old John Wynn poses with the driver, Bill Heywood.

to appear! Following Thomas's death, the business was run by Robert Wynn and his sister Emma. At the time, Robert, one of 10 children, was aged just 15. Within four years, at the age of just 19, Robert had married Nora Small whose father, Samuel, was involved in the extraction of round timber from local forests. Samuel Small died two years later and Robert purchased his father-in-law's business at auction. It was this which started Wynns' 80-year long association with the timber haulage business.

With the rapid expansion of the steelworks at Newport, Robert saw that there were possibilities for providing heavy haulage services. By 1890, he had built a horse-drawn wagon which was capable of hauling 40 tons... with the assistance of 48 horses, harnessed in teams, four abreast! It was also during this decade that Robert introduced steam power into the business, employing Fowler and Garrett traction engines and tractors for loads which did not suit the horses. Continued growth of the business led to the acquisition of premises at Shaftesbury Street, Newport where accommodation for Robert and his wife.

So, alongside the round timber and regular haulage activities, heavy haulage became the third arm of the growing Wynns' business. Like it or not, these heavy haulage activities acquired a high profile and over the years became crucial to the company's success. Wynns' vehicles regularly found themselves being called upon to shift all manner of difficult loads, up to, what at the time was considered a staggering 40 tons in weight.

Like his father before him, Robert sired 10 children and was eventually joined in the business by his five sons, all of whom contributed to the firm's continued expansion.

MOVING GUNS

At the outbreak of the First World War in 1914, some of the company's traction engines were commandeered by the War Office. Nevertheless, Wynns became involved in moving heavy guns and other equipment, and was also able to continue with the extraction of felled timber, going

service this aspect of the business.

The company's first internal-combustion engined vehicle, a 25hp petrol-engined Palladium, was acquired in 1916. Perhaps slightly better known for its motor cars, Palladium was an obscure maker which, until about 1922, assembled trucks in Putney from French components. The second such vehicle, a 59hp Karrier, followed three years later, with a pair of rebuilt ex-WD Subsidy type solid-tyred Albions joining the fleet in 1921 and 1922.

In 1923, the company was incorporated as Robert Wynn & Sons Limited, with the capital shared equally between Robert and his wife, Nora. When Robert died that same year, his share was divided equally between his three eldest sons, Samuel, Robert Thomas - known as 'RT' to distinguish him from his father, and George. By this time, steam traction engines were being phased out and were replaced by Sentinel steam wagons... the maker, incidentally, always insisting on the spelling 'waggons'... along with a single Foden

being the first mechanically-propelled articulated vehicle in the country.

With these vehicles, Wynns initiated regular runs to London carrying tinplate from the Mellingriffiths Tin Plate works at Whitchurch, Glamorgan and bringing back foodstuffs. Further expansion saw the opening of a depot at Cardiff, run by 'RT'.

Percy Wynn, who had been apprenticed to Fowlers, joined the business in the early 'twenties.

Although the Foden already referred to had been the company's first articulated vehicle, the days of steam haulage were clearly coming to an end. Weight restrictions introduced in the 'Road Traffic Act' of 1930 reduced the useful payload below break-even and this finally brought an end to the dominance of steam. The company's first Scammell, a solid-tyred chain-driven tractor-trailer combination, had been acquired in 1927 but eventually there were 30 petrol-engined Scammell Six-Wheelers providing nightly long-distance trunk services between Newport, Cardiff and

Although it was difficult for civilian operators to acquire new vehicles during WW2, Wynns took delivery of three ERF tractors during 1941. The photograph shows Wynns' number 103 (CDW 917); the others were numbered 101 and 102 (CDW 909, CDW 910). Note the very modern wheels on the semi-trailer.

Wynns' Scammell number 51 (KH 9895) was a 45-ton tractor which had been bought new in 1929 by G Earle.

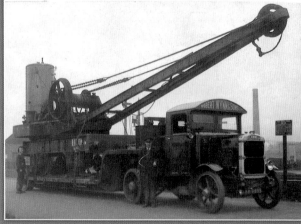

Scammell 51 with a Cardiff-built Patton steam crane on a low-loading trailer.

Garrett under-type six-wheeled steam lorry. Garrett's first six-wheeler was constructed in 1926; this example was delivered new to Wynns in July 1929 and was numbered 42 in the fleet (DW 6616).

Seen here in its intended role, this Foden DG4 4x2 timber tractor (Wynns' number 104, CDW 919) was another WW2 acquisition.

London. These 30-foot long trucks were capable of carrying 13 tons which, at that time, was a considerable load. Indeed, so important was this aspect of the business that Gordon Wynn, the fifth and youngest of the brothers, moved to London to manage operations from that end of the route.

A number of the steam-powered vehicles remained in service for local tar-spraying contracts, road-laying for Cardiff City Council. The steam from the boiler was piped around the tarpot to keep the tar liquid.

During this period, heavy haulage continued to provide a glamorous aspect to the business, and heavy low-loader trailers were built or acquired which allowed loads such as railway locomotives, earth-moving equipment, huge ships' propellers, and industrial plant and machinery to be moved.

In December 1935, Wynns acquired the vehicle fleet of the Pearce Haulage Company, which included a number of heavy Scammells. One of these vehicles, a 45-ton tractor on pneumatic tyres, was eventually rebuilt as a forestry tractor and gave sterling service for a couple more decades. Other Scammells acquired at this time included a 45-ton tractor which had been bought new in 1929 by G Earle. Although it ran on solid tyres, this particular vehicle became an important element of the heavy haulage fleet all through the war years and was not broken up until the early 'sixties.

WARTIME

By the outbreak of war in 1939, the fleet was a mix of steam and petrol-engined vehicles… although it is worth pointing out that a number of horse-drawn vehicles, generally pulling tipper carts, also remained in service right up to the end of the 'thirties. Sentinel steam wagons worked alongside petrol-engined vehicles from Garner, Bedford and Scammell. The heavy chassis produced by the Watford-based Scammell company become increasingly important in Wynns heavy haulage activities and, by this time, the fleet included chain-drive four-, six- and eight-wheeled vehicles, in rigid

John and his sisters pose in front of Scammell number 51.

In 1935, this 45-ton pneumatic-tyred Scammell (Wynns' fleet number 49, DW 9735) was acquired as part of the fleet of the Pearce Haulage Company. Initially used on the road, it was subsequently rebuilt as a forestry tractor.

and articulated chassis form. Many were still wearing solid tyres at the rear since pneumatic tyre technology had yet to develop to the point where the tyres could reliably support extreme loads.

The Second World War provided plenty of opportunity for the company to demonstrate its skill with moving heavy and awkward loads as well as continuing with regular haulage and timber contracts. During this period, Wynns contributed to the war effort, with their vehicles regularly called upon to shift tanks, aircraft, engineer's equipment, machinery, landing craft, and gun barrels.

Although the fleet was not getting any younger, the motor industry naturally gave priority to the military services and

it was difficult for a civilian enterprise, even one with as high a profile as Wynns, to acquire new vehicles during the Second World War. The company did manage to take delivery of three diesel-powered ERF tractors for semi-trailer, and a rare Foden six-wheeled heavy drawbar tractor unit, one of only three such machines constructed.

However, the end of the Second World War, and the subsequent availability of war-surplus Scammells, Pacifics and Diamond Ts, ushered in what many consider to be the most interesting period in the Wynns story. Re-engined and rebuilt more than once in the company's own workshops, these old warriors gave sterling service for another 30 years.

Until the purchase of the massive Diamond T and Pacific tractors after the war, of which more in later chapters, Scammells were an important part of Wynns' heavy-haulage fleet. This 45-ton 4x2 chain-drive tractor (Wynns' fleet number 87, CDW 33) was purchased new in November 1938.

Although originally running solid tyres at the rear, the tractor was subsequently converted to pneumatics all round. Note how the solid-tyred step-frame semi-trailer has been extended by the addition of a separate bogie, using the load to provide structural rigidity. Steering must have been a nightmare!

Truck stop

John Wynn, with his back to the camera, and Mike Lawrence discuss the finer points of operating Mike's ex-Wynns Pacific. Dubbed the Dragon Wagon by its US Army crews, the Hall Scott-engined Pacific TR1 was designed by the Knuckey Truck Company of San Fransisco and employed their massive chain-drive rear bogie. Its original role was to recover disabled tanks under fire but Wynns Heavy Haulage found the machine to be ideal for its brand of heavy haulage.

WHO DARES WYNNS! PART TWO

THE D...

John Wynn and Pat Ware take a look at the early post-war activities of the legendary heavy-haulage company Robert Wynn & Sons

John Wynn and driver Rex Evans (Rex generally drove number 195) pose in front of three Cummins-powered Pacifics - Dreadnought, Conqueror and Helpmate - (fleet numbers 192, 193, 196; GDW 277, HDW 122, GDW 585). The trucks were constantly modified in Wynns' workshops in response to experience gained in service and, as well as receiving new engines, all have been fitted with new cabs and steel ballast bodies.

We have already recounted the story of the early years of Robert Wynn & Sons, starting in 1863 when Thomas Wynn established himself as a carrier in Newport, South Wales. Having followed the company's activities through to the end of WW2, now we take a look at the ex-military vehicles which proved to be so vital in the consolidation of Wynns reputation for heavy haulage expertise in the post-war years.

The decade following the end of WW2 was a time of great change in the UK road haulage industry. Nationalisation of the industry had started in 1947, and some of Wynns' trunk routes were turned over to the newly-nationalised carriers. However, the company managed to largely escape the fate which befell so many of the industry's well-known names because the percentage of exempted traffic which Wynns carried meant that the heavy haulage and round-timber work was able to remain in private hands. Within a few years, Wynns, and the nationalised Pickfords, were the only companies offering heavy-haulage services, and the former quickly expanded its operations so as to be able to compete with Pickfords across the entire country.

HEAVY HAULAGE WAS ENJOYING AN UNPRECEDENTED BOOM.

There was enormous demand for heavy-haulage services during the 'fifties and 'sixties as the country started to modernise industries which had been decimated by the long years of war. For example, the Central Electricity Generating Board (CEGB), which had been established in 1948, struggled to build sufficient generating and distribution capacity to accommodate the increasing demand for electricity. At the same time, there was much rebuilding and expansion of the nationalised gas, coal and steel industries and, at times, it must have seemed that huge transformers, generators, fractionating columns, boilers, and stators were criss-crossing the country as Wynns and Pickfords crews struggled to manoeuvre massive loads along the, as yet, unmodernised British road network.

AMOND &
PACIFIC YEARS

At least one of Wynns' Diamond Ts (fleet number 199; HDW 107) had the big steel ballast body removed, and was converted to fifth-wheel form. It is seen here hitched to a low-loader trailer carrying 45-ton diesel-electric locomotive bound for Australia.

Here's how the Diamond T looked when in the careful ownership of the British Army... this is the closed-cab Model 980 without the winch fairlead rollers in the front bumper.

A pair of Diamond Ts, both still with their ballast bodies, negotiate a 100-ton ingot buggy on a solid-wheeled trailer across the railway tracks at the Steel Company of Wales, Abbey Works at Margam, Port Talbot. Dating from 1949, the trailer lacks the hydraulic steering which appeared a couple of years later making life so much easier when handling huge loads on narrow roads or in confined spaces.

Unfortunately, heavy prime movers, suitable for shifting these exceptional loads, were in short supply and Wynns was forced to turn to the war-surplus market for suitable vehicles, buying American-built Diamond T and Pacific tractors and adapting them to suit their particular requirements. But what a treat they turned out to be!

DIAMONDS ARE TRUMPS
Both the British and US Armies used Diamond T tractors in the tank-transporter role during WWII and, whilst watching a convoy of these vehicles on the Cardiff to Newport road, HP Wynn was apparently hugely impressed when one of the convoy was forced to brake hard. The air-assisted braking system allowed the truck to lock-up all of its wheels and leave tyre tracks along the

Photographed at the US Army's Engineering Standards Vehicle Laboratory at Detroit in September 1944, this is how the Pacific Dragon Wagon looked in its dress uniform... weighing in at more than 37.5 tons. In Wynns' ownership, the armoured cabs were stripped off... reducing the weight by around 10 tons!

The Glory Days of Heavy Haulage

British truck could match. In fact, he was apparently so impressed that he resolved the company would, one day, own and operate some of these tractors.

The Diamond T was the result of a 1940 British Purchasing Commission requirement for a ballast-bodied draw-bar tractor which could supplement the Scammell Pioneer tank transporter. The latter was never available in sufficient numbers and, anyway, lacked the capacity to handle the ever-increasing weight of WW2 tanks. Several US truck manufacturers had been approached as possible suppliers, but it was the Chicago-based Diamond T company that was eventually chosen. The vehicle which they produced was described as the Model 980 (the 981 differed only in having winch fairlead rollers at the

12-ton Model 512.

In common with many US manufacturers of large trucks, Diamond T did not build engines and a Hercules DFXE six-cylinder diesel unit was chosen, producing around 200bhp from 14.5 litres. Whilst the choice of a diesel unit provided commonality with the Gardner-powered Scammell, it also meant that the Diamond T was one of only a very few diesel-powered trucks in the US Army, which tended to favour petrol. This led to the Diamond T being classified as 'substitute standard' when compared to the later Pacific M26 tractor, of which more anon.

Delivery of the first Diamond T tractors

life, some eventually receiving new cabs as well as Cummins engines in place of the Hercules diesel. The draw-bar configuration proved to be extremely versatile and the vehicles were used solo and in tandem with a whole range of special trailers, but at least one (HDW 107, fleet number 199) had the big steel ballast body removed, and was converted to fifth-wheel form.

A pair of Diamond Ts acting in tandem was more than capable of shifting loads up to 130 tons and these tractors formed the mainstay of the Wynns heavy-haulage fleet for around 25 years, shifting all manner of over-sized and over-weight loads.

John Wynn watches how it's done as Wynns fleet number 160 (EDW 95) inches forward with a huge transformer. Note the US Army M1A1 Kenworth or Ward LaFrance heavy wrecker at the rear... more on this in next month's instalment.

Much rebuilt, most notably with a new cab, front bumper and Cummins engine, Diamond T Model 981 (fleet number 91; 3630 DW) hauls a 100-ton excavator through Pontypool town centre. A second Diamond T can just be seen pushing at the rear. The tiny badge on the radiator grille, beneath the Diamond T emblem, reads 'Cummins Diesel'.

was scheduled for 1941 and by the time the war was over, around 6,000 of these superb vehicles had been produced. The stylish 'art deco' cab, with its outrageous V-shaped windscreen had given way to the standard military-style open cab in August 1943, but otherwise there were few changes and the truck was described by the military as being 'most reliable'.

The standard trailer was a multi-axle 40-45 ton design manufactured by Cranes, Dyson and a number of other companies in the UK, with similar designs produced by Rogers, Fruehauf, Winter-Weiss, and Pointer-Williamette in the USA.

With the war finally out of the way, Diamond Ts started to appear on the surplus market and the first two were acquired by Wynns in 1947. Registered EDW 95 and EDW 96 (Wynns fleet numbers 160 and 161), these two trucks were the first of a total of 30 of these splendid machines which were eventually acquired, along with a number of the matching trailers. With their economical... well, relatively economical... diesel engines, Wynns were able to put the Diamond Ts to work straight away.

All of the tractors were continuously

THE DRAGON WAGON

In 1950, Wynns' Diamond Ts were eclipsed by another ex-military vehicle... the incredible Pacific M26, dubbed the 'Dragon Wagon' by its US Army crews.

When Japan's attack on Pearl Harbor encouraged the USA to joined the War in 1941, the only heavy tank transporter available to the US Army was the Diamond T but the US Army was unhappy with the vehicle for a number of reasons. Firstly, it was diesel powered and no comparable US trucks at the time were fitted with diesel engines. They would also have preferred a fifth-wheel machine with a higher rating to accommodate the increasingly-heavy tanks coming out of the tank arsenals. It was also unarmoured and so was not suitable for operation in combat areas... and lastly, it was in short supply.

The US Army started looking for an alternative tractor-trailer combination for the transportation and recovery of tanks, on and off the battlefield.

One vehicle put forward for possible evaluation was a huge forward-control tractor produced by the Knuckey Truck Company of San Francisco who specialised in custom-built heavy-duty off-

The Glory Days of Heavy Haulage

and quarrying applications. Based on the chassis of an existing Knuckey truck, the vehicle featured an armoured-cab, and was coupled to a Fruehauf 45-ton semi-trailer with folding loading ramps at the rear which, the later production form, bridged the trailer wheels.

The machine was powered by a Hall-Scott 400 engine, a monstrous six-cylinder petrol unit producing 240bhp from its more than 17.5 litres... and with some 800 lbf/ft of torque available. This power unit, which had been introduced by Hall Scott in 1940, and was described as 'the most-powerful truck engine built', was coupled to the patented Knuckey centre-pivoted walking-beam rear bogie via a four-speed Fuller gearbox and three-speed transfer case, with final drive by massive chains. The maximum road speed - without load - was 26mph and the truck was enormously thirsty, consuming fuel at a rate of just 1.08 miles per gallon.

Although Knuckey's involvement in the project continued through the supply of the massive rear bogies, production was entrusted to the Pacific Car & Foundry Company, and some 1372 of these monster machines were produced between 1943 and 1945. The armoured version was replaced by a soft-skin variant in 1944, with a further 800 or so constructed and the trucks were used almost exclusively by the US Army.

The Pacific saw service in Normandy and in the advance across Europe but, inevitably, some of the tractors never left these shores and, in 1950, Percy Wynn learned that a number were available for sale... from a quarry in Kent! He purchased six at a cost of £400 each, swiftly followed by four more for parts, and apparently recovered the purchase cost by stripping off the armoured cabs and selling the high-grade steel for scrap.

It was Percy's intention that these huge tractors would be able to handle over-sized loads which were too big even for the Diamond Ts but the high fuel

Bereft of its nameplate, Dreadnought (192, GDW 277), coupled to a hydraulically-steered and suspended trailer, negotiates a 100-ton 60kVA transformer around a tricky corner en-route to Plymouth. The advent of hydraulic steering meant that a pusher truck at the rear was no longer required to assist in manoeuvring the load. The date is probably late 1951; note the opening windscreen which is not apparent on later photographs.

The M26A1 was a soft-skin version of the Dragon Wagon. Here John poses alongside 'Lot 367', one of two vehicles purchased at auction. The same type of Hall Scott petrol engine was originally fitted to both variants.

consumption was a serious disadvantage. The remedy lay in replacing the thirsty Hall Scott engines with a more economical diesel unit and the trucks were rebuilt in Wynns' workshops as they were required for service, with the petrol engines initially ousted in favour of Hercules DFXE engines taken from Diamond Ts and latterly, turbo-charged Cummins units. At the same time, the manual Fuller gearboxes were replaced by semi-automatic units which gave easier changes and reduced the shock loading on the driveline. The military fifth wheel was removed and replaced by a small ballast body, allowing the trucks to be used with drawbar trailers, and the cabs were also rebuilt. On some tractors, the original military wheels were comprehensively reinforced, presumably as a result of experience... but the distinctive chain drive remained... and the Pacific was the first of the Wynn's vehicles to feature power steering!

As the six Pacifics gradually entered service... a process which, incidentally,

John and Percy Wynn (the latter with his inevitable trilby hat) watch as a Pacific Dreadnought (192, GDW 277) manoeuvres a huge crane girder bridge en-route to Uskmouth Power Station.

took almost 15 years... they bore little resemblance to the brutal military machines which had been turned out of Pacific's railway works in Renton, Washington.

John Wynn, who would have been just 18 when the first Pacific entered service in late 1950, took it on himself to name the tractors, selecting the names *Dreadnought* (Wynns' fleet number 192, GDW 277), *Helpmate* (196, GDW 585), *Conqueror* (193, HDW 122), *Challenger* (195, YDW 356), *Valiant* (194, 1570 DW) and *Enterprise* (197, ADW 228B). The last named, which has survived into preservation in the ownership of Mike Lawrence, did not enter service until December 1964.

Powerful, distinctive and always immaculately turned-out, the Pacifics became something of a legend over the years.

The first, and perhaps the most eye-catching load to be associated with these monsters was a 105-ton North British locomotive intended for the Indian State Railways. Without the resources to actually undertake the project Percy Wynn effectively took the contract from under state-controlled Pickford's nose and only once he had the contract in the bag did he order the steel beams that were required to construct the trailer, a task which took just two months! In April 1951 this locomotive was delivered to the Festival of Britain site on a solid-tyred trailer from the Surrey Docks where it had been brought by ship from Glasgow. The tender was moved by one of Wynns' Diamond Ts. When the locomotive left for the docks in September, for onward transportation to India, it was carried

John Wynn started driving when he was 12 or 13 and spent all his spare time at the Wynns yard.

on a new trailer and one that was a first for Wynns... a 150-ton Cranes unit with pneumatic tyres, and hydraulic suspension and steering, the latter signaling a change in technique as the rear tractor in a push-pull configuration was no longer required to provide steering input.

THIS WAS THE LOAD THAT REALLY PUT WYNNS ON THE HEAVY HAULAGE MAP.

However, the largest and heaviest piece of equipment shifted by one of these incredible machines was a 220-ton transformer which was transported from the English Electric factory at Stafford to Ferrybridge Power Station in Yorkshire. It was carried on a 48-wheeled trailer, using no less than three of the Pacific tractors. A subsequent lift saw four of these tractors move a 212-ton 400kV Ferranti transformer across the Pennines... the steepest section of which took some three hours. The Pacifics were also used in conjunction with Wynn's innovative 'hover' trailers which were developed to reduce axle loadings when exceptional-heavy loads had to be moved across weak bridges.

For some two decades, the Diamond Ts and the Pacifics formed the backbone of Wynns heavy haulage fleet, with several of the latter remaining in service way past Wynns centenary celebrations in 1963.... even into the 'seventies.

The age of the ex-military tractor started to come to an end in 1966 when Wynns, by that time part of United Transport, took delivery of the first of 25 new Scammell Contractors. Initially rated at 100 tons but subsequently up-rated to 150 and then 240 tons, these machines proved themselves to be more than worthy successors to the Pacifics and Diamond Ts.

Pacific Enterprise (197, ADW 228) entered service in December 1964 and, despite a period languishing in a scrapyard, has survived into preservation in the ownership of Mike Lawrence.

John Wynn

John Wynn will need little introduction to most readers of *Classic & Vintage Commercials.*

Born on 28 October 1932, he was great-grandson to Thomas Wynn who, in 1863, had founded the company that became known as Wynns heavy haulage, and son of George ('OG'). Taken under the wing by (Uncle) Percy Wynn, and thus saved from a life of tedium on the administrative side, John started driving at 16 and never really looked back.

Along with his cousin Noel, John joined the board of Wynns in 1960. Following the sale of the company to United Transport in 1964, he stayed with the business until the recession of the early 'eighties saw Wynns merged with Sunters under the name United Heavy Transport. In June 1982 John resigned due to frustrations with the increasing red tape... after 34 years with Wynns this was a step he could never have envisaged taking.

Through a lifetime's involvement with heavy haulage, which continues to this day, John has become something of a legend among transport enthusiasts.

Whilst more than 50 years might separate the photographs, John's obvious enthusiasm for driving remains undiminished.

WHO DARES WYNNS!
PART THREE

OLD S

John Wynn and Pat Ware take a further look at other ex-military vehicles employed by the legendary heavy-haulage company Robert Wynn & Sons

Thornycroft Amazon equipped with a useful Coles 5-ton electro-magnetic crane mounted on a turntable.

During World War 2, the USA produced more than three million soft-skin transport vehicles and under the provisions of the Lend-Lease Act of 1941, supplied vehicles and equipment worth more than $42 billion to more than 44 countries. At the end of the war thousands of vehicles remained in the UK and Europe, surplus to requirements and destined for disposal... the US manufacturers having wisely insisted that surplus vehicles were not repatriated.

Many of the vehicles used by the British during WW2 had come from the USA under Lend-Lease and, as well as keeping thousands of these for the post-war reconstruction of the army, the UK government chose to sell surplus vehicles to other nations. At the same time, many were also made available to civilians and, although some were combat-weary veterans, there were also unissued low mileage examples... and all were available at a fraction of their original cost. Wynns had received some new vehicles during the war under government licence, allowing them to continue with vital haulage work but new civilian trucks were

in short supply and remained so after the war. Not surprisingly, Wynns were not alone in acquiring military-surplus vehicles, adapting them as required for their new role... the company even purchased a pair of Jeeps as support vehicles, one in 1948, the other as late as 1961!

In the previous episode we looked at the charismatic Diamond T and Pacific tractors which had formed the backbone of Wynns heavy-haulage fleet for the two decades following the end of WW2. Although the Pacifics, particularly, should be considered the most significant vehicles operated by the company, they were not the only ex-military vehicles which Wynns acquired. The more mundane old warriors such as AECs, Thornycrofts, Chevrolets and Scammells might have lacked the glamour of their larger cousins, but were equally able to earn their keep at a variety of tasks.

Many of these military trucks were superb machines... simple, rugged and reliable. What they might have lacked in sophistication or looks, they more than made up in performance and value for money. For example, in 1958, Wynns paid auction prices of £680 for a Pacific tractor and £700 for a Diamond T and, over a

OLDIERS NEVER DIE

Left: Pair of Canadian CMP Chevrolet trucks with the distinctive reverse windscreen cab. These are 15cwt 4x4 trucks which have had their rear bodies removed to allow them to be used with pole trailers.

period of 20 years or so, Percy Wynn (and subsequently John Wynn) purchased and operated almost 100 ex-military vehicles. Most came direct from Ministry sales but a handful had already been in civilian hands before being acquired by Wynns.

The Diamond T was certainly the most significant in terms of numbers but other notable vehicles which appeared in the fleet included the AEC Matador, Chevrolet CMP, Foden DG4/6, FWD SU, Scammell Pioneer, Thornycroft Amazon and Nubian, the Ward LaFrance M1A1 heavy wrecker... and, of course, the mighty Pacific. There was also a lone Federal 606 7.5-ton recovery vehicle, the couple of Jeeps already referred to, a blue-painted ex-US Navy Dodge 4x4 ambulance, which was described as a van, a Guy FBAX and a pair of Karrier K6s, one of these latter vehicles was the first so-called 'tackle wagon'. A Bedford QL tanker was also acquired and used as a static yard tanker.

It is almost certainly true to say that without these ex-military vehicle Wynns - and many other haulage companies - would not have been able to survive the immediate post-war years.

Looking as pleased as Punch, John stands alongside a war surplus Ward LaFrance M1A1 heavy wrecker awaiting disposal at auction. The vehicle to his left is an American Brockway B666 bridge erector.

The Canadian CMP trucks were produced in 8cwt, 15cwt, 30cwt and 3-ton configurations to a common pattern, but each with its own chassis length. This is almost certainly a 30cwt chassis.

AEC MATADOR 0853

The Matador is one of those trucks that seems to have been able to do anything that was thrown at it... it was designed by Hardy Motors in the early 'thirties and was used by the British Army as a medium artillery tractor, a role which it performed admirably throughout WW2 and into the post-war years – in fact it was so good that there was also a post-war version. It even saw some military service as a make-shift tank transporter and recovery vehicle. Most examples were powered by AEC's superb 7.58-litre diesel engine driving all four wheels through a four-speed gearbox and two-speed transfer case.

Left: War-time (1942) Foden DG6 drawbar tractor receiving assistance at the rear from a Scammell Pioneer SV2S recovery tractor.

Acquired in 1949, this Dodge WC54 ambulance was originally owned by the US Navy... it served with Wynns as a general-service van and was frequently driven by John who, in those pre mobile phone days, used it for 'knocking-up' the drivers who were required for duty the next day.

This Thornycroft Nubian 3-ton 4x4 truck was not improved by turning over on Blakeney Hill in Gloucestershire!

In civilian hands it found post-war employment as fairground and circus transport, as a bus recovery vehicle, and as a forestry tractor where its high ground clearance, short wheelbase and forward-control cab made it ideal for working in amongst standing trees.

Wynns acquired and operated a dozen ex-military Matadors over a 13-year period, the last appearing in 1971. Like many involved in the round timber trade, Wynns favoured them as timber tractors but latterly, a number were used as tackle wagons, one famously being used to help position the huge guns which to this day grace the entrance to the Imperial War Museum.

CHEVROLET CMP

The so-called Canadian Military Pattern (CMP) vehicles were probably the most successful example of standardised vehicles from the war years. Constructed to a common pattern by both Ford and General Motors (Chevrolet) of Canada, the vehicles

were produced in a range of chassis types ranging from an 8cwt 4x4 to a 3-ton 6x6 and were powered either by Chevrolet's 3.5-litre six-cylinder petrol engine, or the 3.9-litre side-valve V8 Ford. Common cabs were used, making it difficult to differentiate between the products of the two manufacturers.

By the end of the war Canada had produced 815,729 soft-skin vehicles, the majority of which were of the CMP type.

Wynns found that the 3-ton 4x4 could be converted into a useful timber tractor, with a pole trailer carried on a fifth wheel bolted across the shortened chassis. Ten such vehicles were acquired and put to work.

FWD SU

Alongside the heavy-haulage and regular freight business, Wynns remained very much involved in the timber trade until 1965, claiming that they were handling an average of more than a million cubic feet of timber every year.

It was very difficult for civilian operators to purchase new vehicles during the war but this pair of Bedford/Scammell tractor-trailer outfits was supplied under licence in 1942.

FWD SU COE 4x4 timber tractor; note the massive spade anchor at the rear. There was a military timber tractor variant of this truck but this vehicle (and others like it) was almost certainly converted by Wynns from a cargo truck.

Scammell tractors had been used in this context before the war but the company started buying FWD trucks in about 1950. The American FWD company had supplied several versions of this 5-6 ton 4x4 tractor, principally under Lend-Lease to the British Army in 1942. With a powerful Gar Wood winch behind the cab, the Cummins diesel-powered CU was originally equipped as a timber tractor; the SU was bodied as a cargo vehicle, auger drill and artillery tractor, and was powered by a Waukesha engine; and there was also a tractor version for semi-trailer. All featured permanent four-wheel drive.

Wynns purchased 10 examples of either the winch-equipped artillery tractor or, possibly, the more-numerous cargo-bodied variant, removing the steel cargo bodies and equipping the chassis either with a simple folding-jib crane for timber extraction, or as a tractor for use with a pole trailer. With its short wheelbase and forward control cab providing excellent

visibility and manoeuvrability, the SU proved itself ideal for this application, and the all-wheel drive also helped to provide additional traction on muddy or steep forest tracks.

SCAMMELL PIONEER

The heavy-duty Scammell trucks had always been important to the company. The first had been acquired back in 1928 and Wynns continued to buy the products of the Watford-based Scammell concern right up to the end.

During the war, Scammell had produced thousands of their 6x4 Pioneer chassis for use as artillery tractors, recovery vehicles and tank transporters. Originally introduced in 1928/29, the Pioneer was the first truck to incorporate Oliver North's innovative walking-beam gearcase and centrally-pivoted front axle which gave it such a formidable off-road performance. Perhaps more important from Wynns' point of view was the low ▶

Originally constructed as the tractor for a 30-ton tank-transporter train, this Scammell Pioneer TRMU30 entered service with Wynns in 1947 and was the last of three such vehicles on the fleet. The driver was Bill Bennett... who also appeared in the photograph of John and his sisters in an earlier instalment.

AEC Model O853 Matador, similarly converted for use as a timber tractor, presumably by Nash & Morgan, outside whose works it poses. The Matador started life as a medium gun tractor.

Above: For some unaccountable reason, this AEC Matador, which was acquired in 1966, finished up being fitted with a Gardner 6LW engine and the radiator from a Scammell Highwayman. The original AEC cab has also been rubber glazed but the finished appearance is surprisingly attractive.

low gearing which enabled the driver to literally inch the vehicle along in the first of its six speeds with the Gardner 6LW engine at little more than tick-over... there was no auxiliary box but there was no need... the overall gearing in first was 181:1!

When surplus Pioneer tank transporters came up for sale in 1946/47, Wynns purchased two of these to supplement the pre-war Scammells which were beginning to show their age, together with one example of the recovery tractor.

The army had used the Pioneer with a purpose-designed 30-ton semi-trailer, attached by means of a semi-permanent sprung coupling, but Wynns chose to remove the fifth wheel, constructing a simple ballast and equipment box behind the original crew cab. With the addition of a heavy-duty hitch, the old Pioneer could haul an ex-military 40/45-ton multi-wheeled drawbar trailer... the very type of trailer that had been designed for use with the Diamond T, and which was constructed by a number of British companies, including Cranes, Dyson, British Trailer Company, Hands, Shelvoke & Drewry and SMT.

The trucks were reliable, if a little antiquated, and there were no further purchases. Possibly because The Pioneers did not compare favourably to the Diamond Ts and Pacifics which became available later, and which started to appear in the fleet from 1950.

THORNYCROFT NUBIAN

Rated by the British Army at a modest 3 tons, the wooden-bodied Thornycroft Nubian TF/AC4/1 cargo truck was typical of British logistical vehicles of WW2 and the company produced around 5000 of these petrol-engined all-wheel drive trucks between 1940 and 1945.

Eight ex-Ministry Nubians were acquired by Wynns between 1956 and 1961; most were used as tackle wagons but at least one, DUH 701, was equipped as a timber tractor.

THORNYCROFT AMAZON WITH COLES CRANE

Originally purchased by the RAF, the Thornycroft Amazon WF/AC6/1 carried a useful Coles electro-magnetic crane mounted on a

One of seven Ward LaFrance M1A1 heavy wreckers as rebodied in Wynns workshops.

turntable. The hoisting, slewing and derricking actions were motor driven via a direct-current generator, and automatic electro-magnetic brakes were provided to control these functions. The generator itself was driven from a power take-off on the main gearbox.

The crane could operate through 360°, and was rated to lift 5 tons at a 7ft radius.

Three of these useful vehicles were added to the fleet, the first was acquired in 1950, with the second and third examples following in 1957 and 1960. The only downside was that the petrol engine was a mite thirsty but since they were only used for general lifting and recovery work this was not a serious problem.

WARD LAFRANCE/KENWORTH M1A1 HEAVY WRECKER

Another of the heavy US Army trucks which saw service with Wynns was the so-called 'M1A1 heavy wrecker'. Introduced in 1943 and constructed in identical form by both Kenworth and Ward LaFrance, the M1A1 was the US Army's standard heavy recovery vehicle, equipped with a Gar Wood 5-ton swinging boom crane, a 17.5-ton rear winch and a 10-ton front winch. The huge angular front bumper was ideal for pushing disabled vehicles.

In its original form, the truck was powered by a Continental 22R 122bhp six-cylinder petrol engine of 8.2 litres driving all three axles via a five-speed gearbox and two-speed transfer case; the front axle could be disengaged when not required. In an attempt to improve the seriously scary fuel consumption Wynns fitted Gardner 5LW or 6LW diesel engines. The maximum speed with the petrol engine had been 45mph and, whilst this won't have been improved by the use of a Gardner, it was more than adequate at a time when heavy trucks were restricted to 20mph on British roads.

With its no-nonsense military appearance and open cab, the truck was unlikely to win any beauty contest prizes but the boys in Wynns' workshop fitted a new enclosed cab, constructed a useful equipment body at the rear, and welded a huge open-jawed coupling on the front bumper.

In all, Wynns purchased seven of these trucks, finding them ideal for recovery work, or acting as an additional pusher, or even as the lead tractor, in a convoy when the going got tough.

EX-MILITARY VEHICLES ACQUIRED BY WYNNS, 1946-71

AEC MATADOR	PDW 42, RDW 65, YDW 22, 906 DW, 1443 DW, BDW 219B, BDW 367C, FDW 636D, GDW 347E, GDW 348E, SDW 948J, WDW 542K
BEDFORD QL TANKER (not registered)	
CHEVROLET CMP	EDW 5, EDW 93, EDW 94, EDW 97, EDW 241, EDW 481, FDW 385, FDW 386, EVJ 805, GDW 192
DIAMOND T 980/981	EDW 95, EDW 96, EDW 868, FDW 533, FDW 922, GDW 313, GDW 800, HDW 107, HDW 562, HDW 572, KDW 560, LDW 810, NDW 232, NDW 925, ODW 937, PDW 321, PDW 927, RDW 976, TDW 241, 1300 DW, 3630 DW, BDW 277B, EDW 782D (and others)
DODGE WC54	JC 7958
FEDERAL 606	EDW 242
FODEN DG/4/6	EDW 601, EDW 602, FDW 60, FDW 61, FDW 183, FDW 184
FWD SU	DDW 601, DDW 605, DDW 771, DDW 889, DDW 890, DDW 891, FDW 77, FDW 79, FDW 80
GUY FBAX	DDW 777
KARRIER K6	EDW 710, HDW 249
PACIFIC M26	GDW 277, GDW 585, HDW 122, YDW 356, 1570 DW, ADW 228B
SCAMMELL PIONEER	DDW 495, DDW 496, HPP 814
THORNYCROFT AMAZON	FDW 752, NDW 743, VDW 248
THORNYCROFT NUBIAN	DUH 701, MDW 880, NDW 44, NDW 548, ODW 95, PDW 319, PDW 848, WDW 319
WARD LAFRANCE M1A1	EDW 158, EDW 340, EDW 599, FDW 4, FDW 216, 3624 DW, GDW 349E
WILLYS MB JEEP	EDW 767, 448 AFC

John Wynn's sons Robert and Peter... proud owners of a Jeep, although obviously not the one of the two Jeeps which appeared on Wynns' fleet list.

Right: This is how the AEC Matador looked in its original artillery tractor form. The lot number on the cab front suggests that this vehicle has just been brought from the auctions.

WHO DARES WYNNS!

THE CHAL... NATION...

PART FOUR

John Wynn and Pat Ware take a look at the company's activities during the 1950... and consider the effects of nationalisation

Rare bonnetted Guy Invincible from 1961 coupled to a low-loader trailer hauling a crane or dragline excavator. In 1959, Wynns had become South Wales' agents for Guy Motors which gave them easy access to the company's products.

Following the end of the war in Europe in May 1945, Winston Churchill formed a 'Caretaker Government', with the Labour Party as its official opposition. Certain of his popularity and consequent victory, Churchill called a General Election in July of that year. Sadly, he misjudged the mood of the country, and the Labour Party was swept to power with a landslide result. Churchill was relegated to opposition.

With a majority of 180, the new administration focused on the need for greater public ownership of industry, instituting a bold and extensive programme of nationalisation. Industries such as coal mining, railways, steel-making, canals, gas, electricity,

the Bank of England... and road haulage, all of which were described by the Labour administration as 'decaying and unprofitable', were to be nationalised.

The Road Haulage Association (RHA), which represented the owners of the industry, was bitterly opposed to nationalisation, and began to distribute propaganda and put-up posters across the country. A 25-minute film extolling the virtues of private ownership was shown more than 3000 times in halls all over the country, with viewers being asked to sign a petition against the proposed nationalisation. In November 1946, the 'Transport Bill' was put before Parliament, seeking to transfer the railways, canals and most long-distance road haulage into state ownership. However, the RHA's lobbying was

not entirely in vain because on 13 March 1947, the Minister for Transport, Alfred Barnes, told the Standing Committee that he intended to remove the clauses from the Bill which limited the operation of 'C' licensed vehicles. At the time there were three types of licence issued to hauliers: The 'A' licence was for public carriers; the 'B' licence for traders carrying the goods of others as well as their own; and the 'C' licence was used by traders transporting their own goods up to a radius of 40 miles from their operating base.

Although the decision undermined his original objective that all long-distance road haulage would be carried by the proposed state-owned road-haulage company, this is how the Bill was passed into law as the Transport Act 1947.

LENGES OF
ALISATION

The Act established the British Transport Commission, giving it powers to acquire transport undertakings as it felt necessary. However, any transport business which could show that more than half of its income came from exempted traffic was permitted to remain in private hands; such traffic included meat, furniture, heavy haulage, bulk liquids and round timber.

Wynns lost their nightly London-South Wales trunk routes... although they weren't paid any compensation for more than two-and-a-half years. Whilst this state of affairs may have been fine for Wynns who had other work, it can't have been good for other, smaller, operators.

By virtue of having bought a fleet of tankers which had formerly been operated by Powell Duffryn, and then subcontracting them to the newly-created National Coal Board, the company was able to increase their exempted traffic beyond the relevant figure and thus was able to escape the net. Many of their competitors were less fortunate and were absorbed into the Pickfords undertaking, which had merged with Carter Paterson in 1946 to form Joint Parcels Service, and which, itself, had been nationalised in 1947.

Bought new in 1938, and running on solid rear tyres, this 45-ton Scammell tractor operated throughout the war and well into the post-war years as part of the heavy haulage fleet.

This Scammell draw-bar tractor dates from 1954 and is acting as back-up to one of Wynns charismatic Diamond Ts to move this boiler or pressure vessel. Note the pneumatic-tyred heavy-duty trailer, typical of the equipment being acquired during this period.

Nationalisation of the selected industries continued apace and, by 1951, 20% of the of the national economy was controlled by the state, employing a workforce of over two million. Whether or not these moves were approved by the majority of the electorate is a moot point but the Labour government was ousted in that same year in favour of a new Conservative administration led by Winston Churchill. The programme of nationalisation was halted, but little on the ground changed, and Wynns, which had always remained in private hands, and the previously-nationalised Pickfords, still had the heavy-haulage field all to themselves

until they were joined by just one other company - Sunters of Northallerton - in the late 'fifties.

Competition between Wynns and Pickfords was fierce and, as previously recounted, Percy Wynn was delighted to be able to snaffle the contract for delivering the 105-ton Indian railway locomotive to the Festival of Britain, even if it did mean that the company had to design and build a pair of necks and carrying beams for the trailer which was built by Fairfields at Chepstow in just two months. The high profile and prestigious nature of this contract, more than anything helped to put Wynns firmly on

the map as an extremely capable haulier, able to deal with heaviest and most difficult loads.

At the beginning of the 'fifties it was

For some time Wynns operated a large fleet of tippers and earth-moving equipment. From left to right, Guy, Dodge and Fordson... the 'dozer is an International Harvester product.

Left: The WD-fronted Bedford on the left was delivered in December 1945 whilst the civilian styled truck on the right dates from April 1946. Both would have become redundant when Wynns lost much of their day-to-day light haulage work.

Below: Photographed in the procession which formed part of Wynns' centenary celebrations, this Guy Warrior is coupled to an ex-WD 'Queen Mary' trailer, designed for carrying aircraft fuselages and wings.

In 1963, Wynns celebrated 100 years of business by mounting something of a carnival in their home town of Newport. Ironically, these two vehicles are separated by little more than two decades, the Fowler dates from 1920, the heavily-modified Pacific from 1943/44.

Motor Panels cabbed Guy Warrior tractor (1961) and semi-trailer outfit; the trailer was specially designed to carry loads slung between the frame rails to lower the centre of gravity.

Dating from 1931, these Scammell six-wheelers were operated on the nightly trunk routes from South Wales to London until Wynns had to give them up following nationalisation.

Resplendent in its new red and black livery this Scammell Highwayman tractor was delivered to the company in 1962 and was typical of the vehicles used for moving middle-weight machinery and plant.

standard practice for any outfit hauling an abnormal load to deploy a 'pusher' truck at the rear, not only to help with the weight but also to steer the rear of the trailer which would otherwise tend to cut across corners. Cranes of Dereham had been working on the development of a heavy trailer which would incorporate hydraulic steering and hydraulic suspension, as well as running on pneumatic tyres; an additional bonus of the hydraulic suspension was that it could be used to raise and lower the trailer frame in place of separate jacks. The company had been working with Dunlop, the latter producing a 16.00-20 24-ply tyre which

was rated for a load of 10 tons at 5mph and 7.5 tons at 12mph... with 16 of these tyres, a trailer could carry 120 tons. Cranes showed a scale model of such a trailer to Percy Wynn – and to Pickfords – at the 1951 Commercial Motor Show. At the time, Percy was in charge of vehicle procurement and engineering for Wynns and immediately saw the potential for this development, and insisted that Cranes build such a trailer for Wynns.

Whilst happily accepting the order, neither Cranes nor Dunlop was prepared to offer any guarantee that such a feat was possible at full scale and the operation was,

effectively, undertaken entirely at Wynns' expense. However, Percy had stolen a march on the nationalised Pickfords who needed more time to evaluate the trailer and to raise the necessary paperwork, and it was the procurement of this trailer which effectively put Wynns and Pickfords head-to-head.

Having placed his order, Percy wanted to see the job through and was often to be found at Cranes checking on the progress of the trailer (which was eventually allocated fleet number 333) during construction. John felt that he was equally involved since, despite being just 19 at the time, he was Percy's chauffeur and always ▶

Not the prettiest of trucks, these Guy Invincible tractors date from 1959 and 1960, respectively. Shown here coupled to step-frame trailers which are carrying pressure vessels, they were equally at home with tanker trailers.

On the left is a 7 1/2-ton AEC Monarch dating from 1946, standing alongside is a 1959 Thornycroft acquired from Edward England Limited, fruit and vegetable merchants of Cardiff; note how the Thornycroft shares the same design of Motor Panels cab as the Guy Warrior shown elsewhere.

took him to Dereham, at first driving Percy's Ford V8 Pilot, then a Ford Zephyr Mk 1, and finally a succession of Jaguars, from Mk VII thru' to the Mk X.

But Pickfords eventually followed suit, ordering a similar 16-wheel 120-ton trailer and effectively forcing Wynns to go one better. In 1952, Percy persuaded Cranes and Dunlop to construct a 24-wheel 150-ton version of this trailer. The trailer was used to successfully move six 150-ton transformers from the British Thompson Houston (BTH) works at Rugby to locations around the country where the Central Electricity Generating Board (CEGB) was constructing power stations.

When the CEGB indicated that there was a need for still-heavier loads to be moved, Wynns wasted no time and, this time, came up with a 28-wheel 200-ton trailer, which used a pair of bogies under the swan necks to help carry the load... an idea which Percy had come up with.

For many years the two companies were constantly battling for supremacy. The 200-ton figure remained the practical upper limit until the mid-sixties when

Wynns purchased a 300-ton trailer (fleet number 789) from Cranes running on two eight-row bogies, where the wheels were shod with 8.25-15 tyres; two separate two-row bogies could also be fitted to provide the maximum 300-ton capacity.

THE 'FIFTIES
During the 'fifties Wynns was scarcely short of heavy-haulage work. Transformers, excavators, generators, railway locomotives and sundry chemical plant were being produced all over the country, and there was no shortage of heavy-haulage work... in an ironic twist of fate, Wynns ex-military trucks and trailers were also occasionally called upon to move tanks. New depots were opened at Manchester and Chasetown to augment the existing Newport, Cardiff, and London locations, and there was also a timber-extraction depot at Welshpool.

In 1953, the company's growing expertise in heavy haulage was recognised when they were asked to test and license a pair of Thornycroft Mighty Antar tractors (JDW 48 and 49) together with a Crane

16-wheel trailer similar to fleet number 333. The vehicles were intended for export to Australia where they were to be used for hauling electrical equipment for the Snowy Mountains Hydro-Electric Scheme. One of the most complex water and electricity projects in the world, the Snowy Mountains Scheme captures the waters of the Snowy River and its tributary, the Eucumbene, at high elevations and diverts them inland to the Murray and Murrumbidgee Rivers, through two tunnel systems driven through the Snowy Mountains. The water falls 2500 feet through large hydro-electric power stations which generate peak-load electrical power for New South Wales and Victoria. The scheme took 25 years to complete and was not fully operational until 1974.

During the UK trials, the Antars were used to haul 120-ton stators from GEC at Birmingham to the Uskmouth Power Station which was being constructed in South Wales. The Australian crews were supposed to be gaining experience with running the Antars but, having seen the roads and terrain involved, refused to drive, returning to 'Oz' with no actual driving experience.

Wynns continued to operate a timber extraction business until the United Transport take-over in 1964. This Unipower Forester tractor is typical of purpose-built machinery used for handling heavy round timber... note the Caterpillar tractor on the low-loader trailer and the living van bringing up the rear.

ERF tractor dating from 1978, 14 years after the takeover and well beyond the savage retrenchment of the early 'seventies. It was eventually transferred to Industrial Fuel Transport of Avonmouth.

Although no examples of Thornycroft's Mighty Antar joined the Wynns fleet on a permanent basis, this was a period of acquisition. Last month we looked at the ex-military vehicles which joined the growing Wynns fleet in the immediate post-war years, but other vehicles acquired during this period included more than a dozen Scammell drawbar tractors, some new, some secondhand, including a pair of Mountaineers... as well as 14 Bedford KHTC 8-ton tippers.

From the end of 1959, the company was also appointed as the main South Wales dealer for Guy Motors. Not only did this give them access to some of Guy's prototypes but it also made it easier to acquire production trucks. A number of Warrior, Invincible and Big J tractors and flat-bed trucks were purchased during this period.

CENTENARY

By the end of the decade, Wynns was close to celebrating its centenary and had already started working overseas... more of which in later installments. However, the five Wynn brothers were approaching retirement age and there was some question regarding the ability of John and his cousin Noel to run what had become a sizeable business between the two of them. Road haulage was about to be privatised under Harold Macmillan's Transport Act 1962 but the Conservatives were tired, having been in power for almost all of the 'fifties, and there was a lingering possibility that any new Labour government would resume the programme of nationalisation that had been abandoned in 1951.

If the growth of the 'fifties was to be continued into the new decade, Wynns needed additional capital. One possibility was a flotation on the London Stock Exchange but this would have meant that the family would have to relinquish control and if this were to happen, the directors believed that it would be better to sell the business outright. Pickfords, by now in the hands of the Transport Holding Company rather than the British Transport Commission, would have jumped at the chance but the family was not keen for Wynns to fall into the hands of their erstwhile competitor.

In 1962, the Wynns board of directors started discussions with United Transport who were seeking expansion in the UK road haulage sector. It was not until February 1964, a few months after the company celebrated its centenary with a parade through the streets of Newport, that the sale of Wynns to United Transport was announced. The chairmanship passed to David Lloyd-Jones, with R T Wynn as his deputy. Percy and Gordon Wynn were joint General Managers, and Noel and John were also appointed to the Board. George Wynn elected for retirement but remained on the Board. John also began to take on the role of vehicle procurement from Percy.

At the same time, the Welshpool depot was sold separately, along with the timber-extraction business, and Wynns also withdrew from tipper work, closing the Cardiff depot but the early 'sixties saw expansion of the company's activities, both at home and, increasingly, overseas.

John Wynn

Born on 28 October 1932, John Wynn was the son of George ('OG' Wynn) and great-grandson to Thomas Wynn who, in 1863, had founded the company that became known as Wynns heavy haulage. Taken under the wing by (Uncle) Percy Wynn, and thus saved from a life of tedium on the administrative side, John officially started his driving career at 17 and never really looked back.

John had actually been driving - illegally - since the age of 12 or 13 and spent all his spare time at the Wynns' depot in Shaftesbury Street, preferring this to school sports! He had already driven a six-wheel Scammell trunker to London and, unbeknown to his family, every Saturday for a period of three or four months had been driving a tanker, another Scammell, loaded with sulphuric acid from the Wynns depot to Treforest, Pontypridd and back, a round trip of 40 miles. When this was discovered, he was 'grounded' by his Uncle Percy and the official driver of the truck involved almost lost his job. As a punishment, John was not allowed out in a Wynns vehicle for the next 12 months unless Percy or Gordon Wynn were around to give the nod.

Soon after the Diamond Ts started to enter service with Wynns, John could be found shunting them in the yard and, when he reached the legal driving age, he regularly took a hand at the wheel on a variety of these charismatic tractors. He also says that he spent a fair few hours at the wheel of the Dodge WC54 ambulance which the company used as a service van, 'knocking up' the drivers for their shifts in the days before mobile phones.

Along with his cousin Noel, John joined the board of Wynns in 1960. Following the sale of the company to United Transport in 1964, he stayed with the business until the recession of the early 1980s saw Wynns merged with Sunters under the name United Heavy Transport. In June 1982 John resigned due to frustrations with the increasing red tape and lack of foresight... after 34 years with Wynns this was a step he could never have envisaged taking.

Through a lifetime's involvement with heavy haulage, which continues to this day, John has become something of a legend among transport enthusiasts.

John Wynn (centre) together with Uncles Gordon (left) and Percy (right)... the 1974 Scammell Contractor, 'Talisman', provides a nice contrast with Fowler 5-ton road locomotive delivered new to the company in 1920.

WHO DARES WYNNS! PART FIVE

With the fleet number 188 (and subsequently registered FDW 769E), this was Wynns' first Contractor, a 100-ton drawbar tractor with the full-width ballast body that subsequently proved to restrict rear vision. Photograph taken at Tolpits Lane, Watford.

POWERFUL CONTRACTIONS

John Wynn and Pat Ware take a look at Scammell's mighty Contractor and the effect these tractors had on Wynns final 15 years

A pair of Mk 1 240-ton tractors manoeuvre a 370-ton 144ft long platform reactor which had been delivered by ship from Italy to the Shell refinery at Shellhaven in 1974. The one-mile move, which entailed turning the reactor through a full 360o was carried out for John Mowlem.

In 1966, Wynns' first Contractor appeared on Scammell's stand at the Commercial Motor Show. Scammell eventually became Leyland Special Vehicles but here, at the 1976 Show, 'Superior', a 250-ton Mk 2 Contractor, is being made ready for the opening.

For the two decades following the end of WW2, the Pacific and Diamond T tractors provided the mainstay of Wynns' heavy-haulage fleet. The inevitable ravages of time were kept at bay by a programme of constant modification and it would be fair to say that by the end of their lives these vehicles would have been unrecognisable to their makers.

However, by the mid-sixties, it was obvious that the old warriors were nearing the end of their useful lives. The new owners of the company, United Transport, sanctioned the purchase of a fleet of new heavy tractors. By this time, Scammell and Thornycroft were the only UK manufacturers of such machines... although perhaps it would be more true to say that

Scammell was the only UK producer of heavy tractors. Thornycroft had built their last Mighty Antar in 1963 and, although there was talk of an Antar Mk 4, nothing was ever to come of this. However, it made little commercial difference since both companies were part of the Leyland Group. Scammell had been absorbed in 1955, and Thornycroft, via its association with ACV, in 1962.

Wynns had operated plenty of Scammells in the 'thirties, and had also purchased a handful of medium-sized Scammell tractors after the war for both drawbar and fifth-wheel operation. Unlike Pickfords and Sunters, Wynns had not favoured the Scammell Constructor which had appeared in 1952, nor, despite

trialling such a machine, had Wynns purchased the more-powerful Super Constructor which had joined the range in 1958, still preferring their home-brewed Pacific and Diamond T tractors. But the announcement of Scammell's magnificent Contractor in 1964 coincided with the need to replace the ageing American machines.

The Contractor was intended to replace the Constructor. It was Scammell's most-powerful tractor to date, as well as being the most successful heavy tractor produced by the company.

Designed for towing either drawbar or semi-trailers, the 'baby' of the range was rated at 100 tons, with 125/150 and 240-ton versions also available, the latter identifiable by its larger rear hubs ▶

This is the largest load which Wynns carried on British roads. One of three enormous pressure vessels which were moved 17 miles from Cammell Laird at Birkenhead to the Shell refinery at Stanlow in a most impressive convoy. The move was effected using double-width six-axle bogies under each end of the vessel, with a Contractor at each end.

'Adventurer', a 150 ton, Mk 1 tractor from 1967 coupled to an ex-MoD tank transporter trailer. Rated at a modest 40 tons, these trailers provided a useful facility for medium loads.

and heavier-duty tyres. During its near 20-year production life the Contractor was offered with Rolls-Royce and Cummins engines rated from 300 to 450bhp and with manual, semi-automatic or automatic transmissions; one intrepid operator even specified a Detroit Diesel engine but, wisely, Wynns chose to stick with Cummins.

It was also a turning point for both companies and led to collaboration between Wynns and Scammell.

FIRST CONTRACTOR

The first Wynns' Contractor, fleet number 188 (FDW 769E), and one of four 100-ton tractors purchased over a two year period, was delivered in 1966. Resplendent in its Wynns livery, the vehicle appeared on the Scammell stand at the 1966 Commercial Motor Show where it attracted huge attention.

And what a fine piece of work the Contractor was... coupled together, two or three of these powerful and capable machines could easily haul more than 300 tons or more. Indeed, in his book Scammell the Load Movers from Watford, Nick Georgano reports that Highland Fabricators of Ross-shire regularly used a pair of Contractors to move loads of up to 1,600 tonnes over short distances!

Early Contractors were powered by a 12.17-litre Rolls-Royce Eagle diesel engine, with the option of a Cummins NT 335 or the more-powerful NT380 and most were constructed in 6x4 configuration. with the massive rear bogie driven through either a Fuller 15-speed gearbox, or an eight-speed Self Changing Gears RV30 semi-automatic unit in combination with an optional two-speed epicyclic splitter which gave the driver 15 very-closely-spaced ratios to play with.

Ro-Ro ferries reduced the need to transport large and indivisible loads long distances by road. It became common practice to shift the load (and the tractors) by sea to the nearest port, only completing the journey by road. Here, 'Challenger', a 240-ton Mk 1 from 1969, shows of a pair of Wynns' multi-axle bogies.

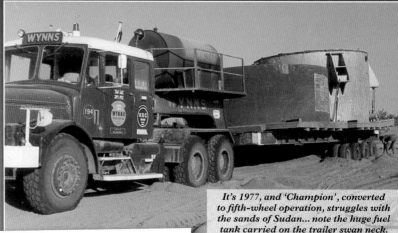

It's 1977, and 'Champion', converted to fifth-wheel operation, struggles with the sands of Sudan... note the huge fuel tank carried on the trailer swan neck. The contract involved transporting 3000 tons of equipment across 1400 miles; the equipment was intended for the construction of a new sugar refinery.

The axles were 40-ton Kirkstall Forge units with epicyclic reduction gearing in the hubs, and, as regards suspension, Scammell had long since abandoned their innovative walking-beam suspension and the Contractor featured massive inverted semi-elliptical multi-leaf springs.

Wynns' early 100-ton vehicles, and most of the 150-ton vehicles, were fitted with a Motor Panels two door cab, seating three across, but later vehicles were fitted with four-door crew cabs capable of accommodating the whole crew of up to eight men. All of Wynn's Contractors were delivered with ballast bodies for use as drawbar tractors, initially carrying a full-width ballast box which it was soon discovered restricted the rear view. Later vehicles were fitted with narrower bodies which forced Wynns to abandon their customary loose steel shot ballast in favour of Scammell's more conventional cast weights.

A number were subsequently retro-fitted with a fifth-wheel in Wynns workshops for use with a semi-trailer (see table) and may even have also been converted back again.

Photographed inside Wynns' Newport depot in 1974, the brand-new 'Hercules', a 240-ton Mk 1, is made ready for a contract in Zambia, a joint project with the Dutch company Mammoet. Note the air-conditioning unit on the cab roof.

The Glory Days of Heavy Haulage

Between 1966 and 1981, Wynns took delivery of 25 Mk 1 Contractors and, as had become the custom, and in the style of railway locomotives, most of the tractors were named by John himself. The company favoured left-hand drive... perhaps in deference to the kerb crawling lives which these heavy tractors often led or perhaps it was a nod to the similarly-controlled Diamond Ts and Pacifics to which the Wynns drivers had become accustomed... and lets face it Wynns' drivers were unlikely to be doing a lot of overtaking.

GREAT RIVALS

The company's great rivals over at Pickfords also chose to buy the Contractor, taking delivery of their first example in 1967, as did almost any company with aspirations in the heavy-haulage business... including Sunters, Wrekin Roadways, Siddle Cook, and the South Africa based Thorntons who, like Wynns, were ultimately taken into the United Group of Companies. The Contractor was also offered as a tank transporter, with examples certainly supplied to Jordan and perhaps Iran; although none was supplied to the British Army in this role, REME did acquire one which has now passed into preservation.

Wynns were also able to contribute to the development of the more-powerful Mk 2 Contractor and, at this point, it might be worth describing the first Wynns' tractor named 'Dreadnought'... Pacific number 192 (GDW 277). This tractor was rebuilt using a Scammell Contractor chassis and subsequently re-registered as NDW 345G and it was this vehicle which led Wynns' engineer Stan Anderson to order a Contractor in the mid-seventies to be delivered without engine and transmission. Having gained experience with the hybrid Pacific/Scammell, Stan intended to produce a more-powerful customised truck which would better suit the company's needs. In the end the Contractor Mk 2, as it became known, was developed jointly by Wynns and Scammell and, despite being rated at a conservative 250 tons, with its 450bhp Cummins engine and Allison automatic gearbox, it was more than capable of hauling up to 450 tons. Interestingly, the Mk 2 lacked the normal Jacobs engine brake (the so-called 'Jake brake') but used a pedal-operated retarder instead. This demanded an unusual driving technique which involved the driver revving the engine on downhill stretches to engage the brake!

Only six Mk 2s are said to have been constructed; four going to Wynns and two to Pickfords.

Until the general downturn of the late 'seventies, Wynns' Contractors were never

'Renown', 240-ton Mk 1, is one of three Wynns' Contractors to have survived into preservation.

As yet unfinished, and thus unrecognisable ('though possibly fleet number 189 or 190 judging by the air cleaner and light configuration), one of the original 100-ton wide-bodied Mk 1s stand outside John Wynn's house... now he must have had tolerant neighbours!

short of work... stators, transformers, railway locomotives, excavators, chemical plant, bridge sections, concrete beams, and all manner of industrial plant. If a heavy or unusual load needed moving... anywhere in the world... then Wynns were in a position to do it.

One particularly interesting load was a 220-ton boiler drum destined for Littlebrook 'D' power station. With a length of more than 100ft, the unit was carried on 10-axle front bogies and six-axle rears, with a 240-ton Contractor at each end. Three loads such loads were carried like this.

AIR CUSHION

The air cushion system which had been developed in conjunction with CEGB engineer Rex Farrell to reduce axle loadings on weak bridges, was also pressed into action again, notably on shifting a series of 258-ton GEC-built stators destined for Didcot, Hinkley Point 'B', Hartlepool and Heysham power stations. A dozen 230-ton transformers were delivered to Pembroke and Didcot power stations, using a new end-suspension system which placed the transformer in a drop-frame carrier suspended on a six-axle bogie at either end; a pair of Contractors provided the motive power... albeit at a max 10mph. Another challenging load was a T-shaped pressure vessel with a maximum width of 35ft combined with a length of 66ft... the 108-ton load was easily handled by a single Contractor but the four-mile move on the MoD's Pendine Proof & Experimental Establishment site involved the removal of power lines and sundry roadworks to accommodate the width.

It is also worth describing the largest load which Wynns carried on British roads.

Of course, Wynns were not the only heavy-haulage operators to use Contractors... here a crew-cabbed Pickfords' ballast tractor is seen with a huge electrical machine carried on a pair of multi-axle bogies.

Preserved Wynns' Contractors Renown and Musketeer photographed (with Pickfords' trailer!) at last year's Great Dorset.

Contractor production

A total of 1,257 Contractors were built between 1966 and 1983, with 73 of these sold in the UK... the bulk of domestic sales going to Wynns and Pickfords. Of this total figure, just six were of the Mk 2 version which was eventually superseded, almost by default, by the S24.

In one of those ironic twists of fate that make history such a fascinating subject, it is worth pointing out that, in effect, there was an Antar Mk 4. Under the able direction of Don Pearson, with assistance from John Fadell and Mike Ballard, the combined efforts of Scammell and Thornycroft designers produced what was effectively a 'son of' Contractor and Antar... the British Army's Scammell Commander.

Sadly, by 1987 Scammell succumbed to the world-wide recession and fell into the hands of Unipower with a very restricted product offering.

WYNNS CONTRACTOR FLEET

Fleet no	Registration no	Date	Name	GTW* and configuration	Notes
182	NDW 836G	1969	Conqueror	Mk 1; 240 ton; crew cab, ballast body/fifth wheel	To Sudan
183	JDW 247F	1967	Traveller	Mk 1; 150 ton; small cab, ballast body/fifth wheel	To Sudan
184	NDW 837G	1969	Challenger	Mk 1; 240 ton; crew cab, ballast body	To Wynns Heavy Haulage
185	JDW 147F	1967	Adventurer	Mk 1; 150 ton; small cab, ballast body/fifth-wheel	To Sudan
186	GDW 848E	1967	-	Mk 1; 100 ton; small cab, ballast body	
187	NDW 838G	1969	Crusader	Mk 1; 240 ton; crew cab, ballast body/fifth wheel	To Tanzania, Namibia
188	FDW 769E	1966	-	Mk 1; 100 ton; small cab, ballast body/fifth wheel	
189	GDW 231D	1966	-	Mk 1; 100 ton; small cab, ballast body/fifth wheel	
190	GDW 249D	1966	-	Mk 1; 100 ton; small cab, ballast body	
191	NDW 839H	1969	Supreme	Mk 1; 240 ton; crew cab, ballast body	To Tanzania, Namibia
193	RDW 339M	1974	Hercules	Mk 1; 240 ton; crew cab, ballast body/fifth wheel	To Tanzania, Namibia
194	SDW 173N	1974	Champion	Mk 1; 240 ton; crew cab, ballast body/fifth wheel	To Tanzania, Namibia
195	GTX 211N	1974	Resolute	Mk 1; 240 ton; crew cab, ballast body	To Nigeria, then Wynns Heavy Haulage
196	HHB 361N	1974	Talisman	Mk 1; 240 ton; crew cab, narrow ballast body	To Sudan
198	SDW 545J	1970	-	Mk 1; 150 ton; small cab, ballast body	To Nigeria
200	SDW 937J	1970	-	Mk 1; 150 ton; small cab, ballast body/fifth wheel	
280	TDW 83J	1971	-	Mk 1; 150 ton; small cab, fifth wheel	To Sudan
281	UDW 139J	1971	-	Mk 1; 150 ton; small cab, ballast body	To Nigeria
600	KAX 395P	1976	Renown	Mk 1; 240 ton; crew cab, ballast body/fifth wheel	To Wynns Heavy Heavy Haulage; now preserved
602	RWO 73R	1977	Superior	Mk 2; 250 ton; crew cab, narrow ballast body	To Wynns Heavy Haulage, Econofreight; now preserved
604	OBO 3R	1977	Illustrious	Mk 1; 240 ton; crew cab, narrow ballast body	To Nigeria
628	XAX 512T	1979	Cavalier	Mk 1; 240 ton; crew cab, ballast body	To Wynns Heavy Haulage
631	YAX 165T	1979	Buccaneer	Mk 1; 240 ton; crew cab, narrow ballast body	Ex Wrekin Roadways, to Wynns Heavy Haulage
633	YWO 24T	1979	Musketeer	Mk 1; 240 ton; crew cab, ballast body	To Wynns Heavy Haulage, Econofreight; now preserved
640	DBO 661V	1980	Invincible	Mk 2; 250 ton; crew cab, narrow ballast body	To Wynns Heavy Haulage
-	XFA 217X**	1981	Dreadnought	Mk 1; 240 ton; crew cab, ballast body	Finished in GEC livery
-	DBF 133Y	1981	-	Mk 2; 250 ton; crew cab, ballast body	To Econofreight
-	DBF 134Y	1981	-	Mk 2; 250 ton; crew cab, ballast body	To Econofreight

* Gross train weight; these are Scammell's figures and can be considered to be more than conservative.

** XFA 217X was one of two Contractors finished in GEC livery but does not appear in any of the Wynns fleet records. Since the registration is Staffordshire-based rather than the more usual Newport, it may well have been an ex Wrekin Roadways vehicle. The name 'Dreadnought', of course, was originally used on Pacific number 192 (GDW 277).

Three enormous pressure vessels, which had been built in the Netherlands, were moved 17 miles from Cammell Laird at Birkenhead to the Shell refinery at Stanlow in a most impressive convoy.

Despite the fact that three footbridges had been dismantled on the route and countless 'keep left' signs and other street furniture had been removed in preparation for the 17-mile journey, John took the decision to postpone the job at the least minute pending the procurement of extra bogies from the Netherlands. Two weeks later, with the bogies which had been supplied by Jack Stoof's Infra Transport in the Netherlands, the move went off without a hitch. One of the vessels weighed 212 tons and measured 112ft in length and 25ft in diameter, and the move was effected using double-width six-axle bogies under each end of the vessel, with Contractors both pushing and pulling.

Wynns general transport operations also continued during this period but, sadly there were hard times ahead. The days of Wynns as a family concern had already come to an end but the name was also soon to disappear from everything except the heavy-haulage operation.

The economic difficulties which the UK faced at the end of the 'seventies led to the closure of Wynns Newport headquarters and depot, and most of the vehicles were transferred to a new company based at Stafford, which was formed out of the merger of Wynns and Wrekin Roadways. The new organisation was named Wynns Heavy Haulage of Stafford. There were to be no Wynns involved in this venture; John resigned in June 1982 and his cousin Noel chose to take retirement.

ACQUISITIONS

Wynns Heavy Haulage also acquired at least one, and perhaps two, Contractors (WNT 307S and XFA 217X), which had formerly been the property of Wrekin Roadways. One of these was painted in GEC livery and serviced the remaining contracts from that company's Stafford works. The other eventually passed to Abnormal Load Engineering of Hixon, Staffordshire when that company was formed in 1983.

The merger did not improve things and the worsening financial position led to the merger of Wynns Heavy Haulage with Sunters of Northallerton to form yet another new organisation, dubbed United Heavy Transport... which did at least retain the distinctive red Wynns livery. Within a year this company had merged with Econofreight to form United Econofreight Heavy Haulage but by 1990, this too had been taken over.

Fortunately, ex-Wynns' Contractors Renown (600, KAX 395P), Musketeer (633, YWO 24T) and Superior (602, RWO 73R), and perhaps others, have passed into preservation, while other trucks found useful second lives overseas. One of the Pacifics has also survived, with Mike Lawrence.

John Wynn

John Wynn was born on 28 October 1932. He was the son of George (OG) Wynn and great-grandson to Thomas Wynn who, in 1863, had founded the company that spent its final years as Wynns Heavy Haulage. John was taken under the wing of (Uncle) Percy Wynn, which saved him from a life of tedium on the administrative side, and he officially started his driving career at 17.

In truth, John Wynn had actually been driving - illegally - since the age of 12 or 13 and spent all his spare time at the Wynns' depot in Shaftesbury Street, preferring this to school sports! Soon after the Diamond Ts started to enter service with Wynns, John could be found shunting them in the yard. However unbeknown to the young John, his father and uncle were well aware of what he was up to and had asked a Zurich insurance inspector to quietly check up on his skills. Following this unofficial driving test, John was declared not to be an insurance risk and was allowed to continue with his under-age driving... whilst on private property. When he reached the legal driving age, he regularly took a hand at the wheel and was not averse to taking the driving seat of the Scammell Contractors... developing skills which have not deserted him all these years later.

John also trained as a draftsman which helped with preparing drawings for the Ministry when applying for licences to move unusual loads, and he was also apprenticed in engineering.

Along with his cousin Noel, John joined the board of Wynns in 1960. Following the sale to United Transport in 1964, he stayed with the business until the recession of the early 'eighties saw Wynns merged with Sunters under the name United Heavy Transport. In June 1982, frustrations with the increasing red tape and what he saw as a lack of management brought John to the point of resignation... after 34 years with Wynns this was a step he could never have envisaged taking.

Through a lifetime's involvement with heavy haulage, which continues to this day, John has become something of a legend among transport enthusiasts.

John Wynn rides shotgun on Musketeer. Is he giving the driver a hard time about that Pickfords' trailer?

WHO DARES WYNNS!
PART SIX

First night's halt in Tanzania for the first convoy of equipment for the Kariba North Power Station in southern Zambia. The motor homes and caravans provided comfortable overnight accommodation for the crews.

EXPORT OR DIE!

John Wynn and Pat Ware take a look at Wynn's overseas operation during the 1960s and '70s, most notably in Africa

Photographed in Zambia during the Kariba North Power Station project in 1974/75, John Wynn stands in front of one of Mammoet's Macks... probably a 6x4 DM800. On the reverse of the photograph John has written 'Drove Mack for half a day... not impressed'.

Over the years, Wynns' expertise in moving oversized and difficult loads became legendary, and word of the company's abilities began to spread around the world.

Not surprisingly, this was followed by requests to become involved in overseas operations, with the first such project coming in the late 1950s when the company supplied three Diamond T tractors and trailers to

Spain and helped train the Spanish crews in the movement of three large generators. In 1959, Arthur Matthews went to Argentina to supervise the movement and installation of heavy equipment, and trailer number 555 was sold to the company who had commissioned the consultancy. Other contracts followed, for the delivery of oil refinery equipment in Cyprus, and the Pacific tractor 'Helpmate' was shipped to the island together with a suitable trailer.

Plenty more overseas work followed over the next decades. During the 'sixties, the civil-engineering company Balfour Beatty was the senior consultant in the construction of the Niger Dam at Kainji. The scheme involved harnessing the rapids near Bussa, with the dam creating a lake which would supply hydroelectric power sufficient for almost half of Nigeria's requirements. Percy Wynn ('HP') had been invited by Balfour Beatty to advise

John Wynn stands beside Pacific tractor 'Helpmate' which was shipped to Cyprus in November 1970 and worked on the delivery of oil-refinery equipment from Famagusta Docks to Larnaca. The truck stayed in Cyprus and was eventually re-registered as FDO 13.

pressed into service again, as was the RRT. At Onitsha the offloading operation was particularly tricky since the barge was unable to approach the ramp head-on due to a combination of low water level and the presence of a sunken ferry, the latter a casualty of the Biafran War which the authorities had failed to disclose to Noel during his 'recce' for the project.

Within a year, the company was over on the other side of the world, shipping what were effectively palletised loads to the USA and Canada via Atlantic Container Lines... on one occasion traveling on the ill-fated *Atlantic Conveyor* which would eventually be lost in the Falklands. One load, destined for Allis Chalmers in Pennsylvania, was loaded onto a Cranes trailer in the UK and then hauled to Liverpool by one of Wynns' Scammell

on how the equipment might be moved back in 1960... his visit to Nigeria coming on the very day that independence was announced. Unfortunately, the River Niger was unnavigable and it was obvious that the massive transformers would have to be moved by a combination of road and rail from Apapa Port, Lagos to Kainji. This involved the construction of a new road from the railhead at Mokwa to the dam site 70 miles away, and the design of a special transporter.

'HP' recommended that Head Wrightson of Thornaby and Cranes of Dereham work together on the design of the unique, and hugely impressive, road/rail transporter (RRT) which was subsequently dubbed the 'Yellow Peril' by Wynns' staff who worked with it in Africa. The RRT carried the transformers in a cradle which could be mounted on either road or rail bogies, conversion from one mode to the other being facilitated by hydraulic support legs. Two 150-ton Scammell Contractors were purchased by the Niger Dam Authority and, after a period of trials with the RRT in the UK, were shipped to Nigeria.

TRAINING CREWS

In 1967, Rex Evans travelled to Nigeria to supervise the assembly of the RRT at Lagos docks and to undertake the training of the Italian and Nigerian crews using a mock-up of the transformer. He also used the rig

At the end of the Zambia project, the two older Contractors were shipped to Kenya together with three trailers where they were used on a joint Wynns/Express Kenya project transporting a pair of 75-ton transformers from Mombasa to Gtaru, 400 miles across the Kenyan plains. The tractors were repainted with the cabs in the familiar Wynns red, and the ballast boxes in Express Kenya's colours.

on a proving run to satisfy the Nigerian rail authorities that the project was feasible. After supervising the movement of the first 120-ton transformer from Lagos to Kainji, Rex returned to the UK, leaving the main contractor to deal with the three remaining units.

Four years later, Noel Wynn was in Nigeria discussing the possibility of moving two 140-ton transformers from Apapa to Onitsha and Oshogbo using combinations of barge and road in the first case, and road and rail in the second. The two Scammell tractors, now owned by the National Electric Power Authority (NEPA) of Nigeria and registered locally as LN 8144 and LN 8145, were

Contractors and pushed onto the ship. At Newport News, Virginia, Wynns' partners Lockwood Brothers pulled the trailer off the ship with their own tractor and completed the delivery without any need to unload the trailer. More intriguing were a number of similar trans-Atlantic jobs which entailed delivering over-size loads complete with a Diamond T tractor (fleet number 199) which could finish the delivery at the other end. Only Wynns could have contemplated repatriating a Diamond T to its country of origin... following its original military service and a full working life in the UK.

Rex Evans made more visits to Nigeria between 1972 and 1974, when Mitsubishi Electric contracted Wynns to move 18 140-ton transformers to almost a dozen different locations across the country. Once again, the moves involved a combination of road/rail and road/barge techniques, with the RRT proving its value yet again. Associated Portland Cement Manufacturers also employed Wynns to move 20,000 tons of machinery for a ▶

Wynns worked with Infra Transport of Holland moving this 460-ton stator from the Brown-Boveri works at Mannaheim, Germany to Maasvlak Power Station, Rotterdam using a 19ft-wide Nicolas bogie set belonging to Wynns. To say that 'HP' was unimpressed with the way that the job was handled would be an understatement.

'Helpmate' prepares to leave Famagusta Docks loaded with a fractionating column which is being carried on a riveted Fairfields trailer deck rolling on Crane bogies.

in Tanzania and then transported 1500 miles west to the dam site. A holding area was established at Kafue sidings, south of Lusaka, and around 100 miles from the dam. Equipment was to be offloaded here and held until required by the Yugoslav team constructing the dam.

JOINT FORCES

The contract involved more than 3000 tons of equipment and, believing this to be too much for Wynns acting alone, the company agreed to join forces with the Dutch company Mammoet who would supply three 150-ton trailers, three Mack 895 tractors and one FTF tractor; Mammoet also agreed to provide a fully-equipped mobile workshop, refueling facilities... and a shower! For their part, Wynns brought along a double-neck swan trailer (fleet number 654) to handle the transformers, two 150-ton trailers and four 240-ton Scammell Contractors, two of which were

number of cement plants across Nigeria. The contract was expected to last six years and, with road movements only allowed on Sundays, often across unfinished roads. Tractors, trailers and personnel were brought from the UK; for example, 'Illustrious', one of the 240-ton Scammell Contractors, was shipped to Nigeria 'brand new' for this job, as was 'Resolute', the latter fitted with an experimental torque converter transmission.

NEARER HOME

Nearer home, Dutch haulage contractors Jack Stoof of Infra Transport had asked John Wynn to assist them in moving a 460-ton stator from Mannheim in Germany to the Netherlands. Whilst Infra Transport were in the habit of running trailers side by side to accommodate excess width, it seems that Wynns 19ft-wide Nicolas bogies were perfect for this particular job because the access doorway at the end of the haul was just 19ft 8in wide... a pair of Infra Transport's trailers would have been around 4in too wide! Infra Transport also provided the motive power for the project in the form of a powerful FTF tractor but, when he visited the work in progress, 'HP' was very unhappy at the way Wynns' name was associated with the hotch potch of tractors and equipment that were used on the job.

The year 1973 saw a pair of Wynns Contractors in France where the company had undertaken to move a pair of enormous cylindrical steel struts which had been manufactured by Babcock Atlantique at St Nazaire, and which were destined for a North Sea oil platform at Graythorpe, near Hartlepool; the larger of the two struts weighed 196 tons and measured up at 144ft in length and 20ft diameter. The move required the struts to be loaded onto a RoRo vessel at St Nazaire and then offloaded in the UK and moved seven miles from the dock to Laing's at Graythorpe where the rig was being assembled. The move was effected by a pair of 240-ton Contractors together with two seven-row multi-wheel Nicolas bogie sets.

Wynns undertook what was certainly it largest overseas project to date in 1974/75

This road/rail transporter (RRT) was developed for the Kainji hydro-electric dam project in Nigeria and was used with two 150-ton Scammell Contractors which were purchased by the Niger Dam Authority. The massive transformers were carried in a cradle which could be mounted on either road or rail bogies.

when the company was contracted to move turbine and electrical equipment to the Kariba North Power Station in southern Zambia. What should have been a relatively straightforward project was made more complicated by Ian Smith's 1965 Unilateral Declaration of Independence (UDI) in the former British colony of Rhodesia. The dam was located on the Zambezi river close to the Zambia/Rhodesia border but sanctions imposed on Smith's regime meant that it was not possible to bring the trucks up by road through South Africa and Rhodesia, and John Wynn and Rex Evans flew out to Lusaka with the idea of scouting alternative routes. Checking bridges on the route, the pair were surprised to find themselves under surveillance by the Tanzanian Army who considered that they might be terrorists! It was established that the equipment could be off-loaded at Dar-es-Salaam

brand new. There was also a caravan of Ford Transit motor homes which provided sleeping facilities for the drivers and crew. Escort and night security services were provided for the convoys by the Tanzanian Army and Police Service, travelling in Land Rovers or on motorcycles alongside the trucks. The Wynns crews also included Sunters' personnel since both were now part of the United Transport Group.

Here, the RRT is being transferred from rail to road mode, with the rail bogies being removed and replaced by road-going units.

Seen here in Nigeria, two 150-ton Scammell Contractors haul equipment for a cement works at Shagmu, north of Lagos.

SPEED HELD DOWN

The convoy speed was deliberately held down to around 10mph, which meant that little more than 70 miles could be covered each day, with the trucks starting out around 6.00am and staying on the road until early afternoon when the temperature often reached 100oF. Much to the chagrin of the Dutch crews who believed that the superior turn of speed of the Macks gave them an advantage, the Scammells quickly proved themselves to be the better machine, particularly on the

In Tanzania it was not uncommon to come across sections where the road had collapsed and here Tommy Cromwell guides 'Crusader' and a flat-top trailer around a local Fiat tanker, trying to find sufficient road surface to support the load.

John Wynn is seen here driving the Scammell Contractor 'Hercules' across Zambia with a transformer load, en-route to the Kariba Dam.

John Wynne and Henk Van Wezel (of Mammoet) pose in front of Scammell Contractor 'Hercules' at the start of the first convoy to leave Dar-es-Salaam for the Kariba North Power Station. A 1500-mile journey lies ahead of them.

most challenging part of the job through the Kitonga Gorge in what is now the Udzungwa Mountains National Park in the Southern Highlands of Tanzania. The section involved a five-mile climb with gradients up to 1:10 and, whilst it required all three of Mammoet's Mack tractors to climb through the gorge with a 60-ton stator, Wynns could manage the load with just two Scammells. Just to keep things interesting, there was a half-mile tunnel at the dam site leading to the underground off-loading bay and it needed two tractors to negotiate this section, one pulling, the other acting as a brake.

At the end of the project, the two newer tractors were returned to the UK whilst the older Contractors were shipped to Kenya together with three trailers and were repainted at the premises of Express Kenya in Nairobi. The cabs were finished in the familiar Wynns red, whilst the ballast boxes were painted in Express Kenya's colours since the two companies were collaborating on a contract to transport of a pair of 75-ton transformers from Mombasa to Gtaru, a distance of 400 miles across the Kenyan plains. The transformers had to be carried higher in the trailer frames than normal in order to provide increased ground clearance and at the end of the journey the crews had to carefully negotiate the load down the partially-constructed dam wall into the substation.

In 1977, Wynns became involved in a ▶

Local wild asses take little interest in a passing 240-ton Scammell hauling a 69-tonne mill body from Apapa, Lagos to the Ashaka Cement Works in Nigeria. Although it has been re-registered locally, the fleet number 604 tells us that this is 'Illustrious'

At St Nazaire in western France, Wynns loaded two enormous steel struts onto a RoRo ship. At West Hartlepool, the struts (which formed part of a North Sea oil rig) were unloaded and continued their journey by road.

The largest of the two struts, seen here at the UK end of the job, weighed 196 tons and measured 144ft in length, with a diameter of 20ft in diameter. Leaving the docks at West Hartlepool, the load negotiates the first bend, with Scammell Contractors both pulling and pushing.

huge project in Sudan, transporting 3,000 tons of equipment for the construction of a sugar refinery across 1,400 miles of largely unmade road but, before we take a look at that incredible undertaking, we should mention the 1980 operation in Ghana when Wynns moved ten large-diameter kiln sections and other equipment from Takoradi to Nsuta. The equipment was destined for the production of manganese nodules at an opencast mine at Nsuta. Two new Scammell Crusader ballast tractors were purchased by Taysec, a Ghanaian operation run by Taylor Woodrow, together with an unusual six-row steerable Nicolas trailer on which the axles were spaced 15ft apart to keep the axle loading below 15 tons. With the platform trailer height at 58in, there were inevitable stability problems and this led to some modifications being made to the suspension layout once the kiln sections were loaded. Conditions on the route often required the tractors to be double-headed.

Away from Africa, Wynns became involved in the construction of power stations in Israel in the 'seventies. The Israel Electric Corporation (IEC) had sought advice on design and construction from the UK Central Electricity Generating Board (CEGB) and, since there were no Israeli heavy-haulage contractors capable of undertaking delivery of the equipment from the port to the construction site, had also enquired about this aspect of the job. The CEGB suggested that Wynns and Pickfords be approached but the work went to Wynns since the IEC was reluctant to deal with a nationalised company.

LOADING UP

Equipment was being supplied by the UK, USA and Canada, and the contract involved loading Parsons transformers onto a RoRo ship in the UK, then traveling to Malta where the ship took on US-built generators and Canadian boilers. At Ashod Port, south of Tel Aviv, Wynns unloaded the equipment and delivered it to the power station site. A subsequent contract for a power station midway between Haifa and Te Aviv saw Wynns also becoming involved in the design of the equipment to ensure that it could be carried on the company's largest trailer, number 999. Fears of a Middle East boycott if the company continued to work in Israel eventually saw the trailer sold to a middle man, John Silbermann of Hallet, who subcontracted the work direct to Wynns personnel to enable the project to be completed.

One of the last of Wynns' overseas contracts was on the Marshall Islands in the Pacific where four 46-ton engines and 30-ton alternators were exported to Majuro. The actual work was contracted to Transtec but it was a stipulation of the contract that the actual movement of the equipment on site was undertaken by Wynns' personnel. The company was sub-contracted to Transtec and Pete Collier and Bernard James went over to the Marshall Islands for the job. The same pair also installed generator sets on the Pacific islands of Guam and Guadalcanal, and in the Philippines.

And finally, in 1983, Wynns trailer 304 was used to deliver a number of boilers from Natal to Tutuka and Majuba. A local heavy haulage contractor undertook the final delivery, coupling the Wynns trailer to a modern Pacific tractor. ▬

Looking decidedly the worse for wear, Scammell Contractor 'Champion' moves a steam crane on behalf of the Port Authority at Dar-es-Salaam.

John Wynn

John Wynn was born on 28 October 1932, the son of George ('OG') Wynn and great-grandson to the company's founder Thomas Wynn. John was taken under the wing of (Uncle) Percy Wynn ('HP'), which saved him from a life of administrative tedium, and he officially started driving at 17, driving 'HP' thousands of miles as chauffeur... three or four times a month he also picked up 'RT' at his Cardiff home, driving him to various customers' premises in his Ford Pilot. John also regularly took a hand at the wheel of many of the company's trucks, including Diamond Ts and Scammells... developing skills which have not deserted him all these years later.

This month we have also included a photograph of John with 'Helpmate' in Cyprus but his first 'real' overseas' foray came in 1974 when he joined the Wynns-Mammoet project moving equipment to the Kariba Dam in Zambia. Three years later John became heavily involved in the Sudan contract, initially flying out to Sudan to survey the site and the route along which the equipment would be moved in order to quote for the job. John was with the first convoy which set out on 12 November 1977 and remained a vital part of the project until the last convoy arrived at Rabak on 10 May 1978.

Along with his cousin Noel, John had joined the board of Wynns in 1960. Following the sale to United Transport in 1964, he stayed with the business until the recession of the early 'eighties saw Wynns merged with Sunters under the name United Heavy Transport. In June 1982, frustrations with the increasing red tape and what he saw as a lack of management brought John to the point of resignation... after 34 years with Wynns this was a step he could never have envisaged taking.

Through a lifetime's involvement with heavy haulage, which continues to this day, John has become something of a legend among transport enthusiasts.

WHO DARES WYNNS! PART SEVEN

Scammell Contractors 'Hercules' and 'Champion' side by side in the Wynns' workshops having been overhauled and fitted with fifth-wheel couplings prior to undertaking the Sudan sugar contract.

'IN THE DESERTS OF SUDAN'

John Wynn and Pat Ware examine the operations which Wynns undertook in Sudan in the late 'seventies.

At the end of 1977, Wynns undertook what proved to be their most difficult overseas operation to date, transporting 3000 tons of equipment for the construction of a refinery for the newly-formed Kenana Sugar Company Limited in Sudan. The refinery in question was a joint project between the Sudanese government and Lonhro, the conglomerate run by Tiny Rowland... the man for whom, incidentally, the phrase 'the unacceptable face of capitalism' was coined. The equipment was to be moved in self-sufficient convoys, each consisting of six trucks carrying 180-200-tons, accompanied by fuel and water, living quarters, and road-making, workshop and cooking facilities. Each convoy had to travel across more than 1000 miles of Sudan in temperatures up to 110oF... and the whole contract was completed in a total just 179 days!

The project began in early 1977 when John Wynn flew to Sudan at the request of John Temme, Logistics Manager for the Kenana Sugar Company. In late 1976, John Temme had been visiting his parents in Newport and had talked to his father - who was the Chief Engineer of Newport BC -and knew Wynns well - about the problems he faced in getting the equipment for the new refinery from Port Sudan on the Red Sea coast, to Rabak, south of the Sudanese capital Khartoum. His father had suggested

A brand-new Caterpillar 16G grader was supplied by the Kenana Sugar Company and certainly proved its worth during the contract.

'Champion' passing through a cutting just outside Port Sudan at the beginning of the journey.

that Wynns might be able to undertake the job and John Temme immediately made contact with John Wynn. The two men met to discuss the project and, within days, John was on his way to Sudan to inspect the port facilities and to survey possible routes.

Independent since 1956, the Republic of Sudan is the largest country in Africa, and the tenth largest in the world, with an area of almost one million square miles. To give you some idea of its size, Sudan shares borders with Egypt, Eritrea, Ethiopia, Kenya, Uganda, the Congo, the Central African Republic, Chad and Libya. It is dominated by the River Nile and its tributaries, and the terrain consists generally of flat plains, broken by mountain ranges. The climate is equatorial, with a rainy season which lasts for about three months during July and September in the north, and up to six months, June to November, in the south. The level of rainfall increases towards the south, where there are swamps and rainforest. In the capital, Khartoum, average rainfall varies from more than 6in to around 39in, with most occurring between April and October. Average temperatures in Khartoum range from 60 to 90oF in January, to a staggering 110oF in June.

EQUIPMENT

The equipment was to be delivered across a distance of about 550 miles as

the crow flies, but with an actual round-trip distance of 1350 miles. Starting at the docks in the north-eastern city of Port Sudan, the convoys would move inland, travelling south-west to Rabak in the White Nile Province, about 150 miles south of Khartoum. Although this meant that the journey would start out in the arid north, fortunately it would not be necessary to spend much time in the Nubian Desert, where sand storms, known locally as haboob, can completely block out the sun.

However, clearly, working in Sudan was going to present its particular set of problems, not least of which, the contract would have to be scheduled to avoid the

rainy months. And, having seen the queues at filling stations, John rightly identified that the provision of adequate fuel supplies would also be something of a challenge. When Wynns submitted their quotation on 26 January 1977, it included the proviso that fuel supplies for the convoys would be the responsibility of Kenana.

The standard of the roads in Sudan was also cause for concern and this was accommodated by insisting that the convoys be accompanied by a Caterpillar 16G six-wheeled motorised grader, which would require its own transport, and which could assist the vehicles through soft or otherwise difficult conditions and repair sections of road. This was also the responsibility of Kenana. As regards food, technical support and accommodation, the convoys were designed to be self-sufficient, but a light aircraft was always on hand to assist in the event of an emergency. A number of trucks in the

En-route to Rabak, the whole six vehicle convoy pauses for a routine inspection in the desert.

'Champion', together with a four-axle semi-trailer and over-sized load... this terrain is typical of that encountered away from the made-up roads.

Here, the grader lends a hand to one of the Bedfords which has become stuck in loose sand.

The going was not always easy and bridges were not necessarily available when required. Here 'Hercules', followed by one of the Bedfords, wades across a shallow river.

convoy were painted with the word 'Wynns', writ large on their white-painted roofs to aid recognition from the air.

CONFIRMATION

On 17 April 1977, Wynns received confirmation that they had been awarded the contract and the company started to prepare the vehicles that would be required.

Three 240-ton Scammell Contractors ('Conqueror', 'Hercules' and 'Champion', fleet numbers 182, 193 and 194, respectively) were overhauled in the company's workshops,

One Scammell and two Bedfords waiting to be loaded at Port Sudan.

having the ballast bodies removed to convert them to fifth-wheel configuration, as well as being fitted with substantial sump guards. Both 'Hercules' and 'Champion' had recently returned from their spell in Tanzania and, following the conversion work, were destined to return, almost immediately, to Africa! Resplendent in newly-applied red, black and white paint, and bearing the name Wynns together with specially-designed decals describing the contract, the three tractors also received the British and Sudanese flags on the bumpers and cab roofs.

Smaller tractors were also required for support, and three new Bedford TM 6x4 tractors, powered by Detroit Diesel 8V71 engines, were purchased. Although they were not registered in the UK, the trucks were named 'Diamond', 'Emerald' and 'Sapphire', and allocated the fleet numbers 609, 610, 611. The convoy was completed by the addition of two new 4x4 Bedford KMs, one of which (608) was equipped with a Hiab crane and workshop body, the other (612) being fitted with refrigeration units and fitted out as a 'chuck wagon'. It is interesting to note that Bedford was not the company's first choice, Wynns would almost certainly have preferred to buy Foden, Atkinson or ERF trucks, but none of these were available... Bedford were

able to offer the trucks 'off the shelf' and, as it turned out there was no need for any misgivings since the Luton trucks proved themselves more than capable of what was demanded of them.

The eight trucks, together with three dollies and six two-, three- and four-axle drop-frame semi-trailers, some of the latter fitted with 800-gallon auxiliary fuel and water tanks on the swan-neck above the fifth wheel coupling, were shipped to Port Sudan on Sudan Line's 'MV Nyala'. Two new long-wheelbase Series 3 Land Rover support vehicles were purchased in Kenya in 'knocked-down' form where they were assembled by Express Kenya and shipped to Port Sudan.

WYNN AT THE WHEEL

On 10 November 1977, the Wynns equipment arrived at Port Sudan and, with little time wasted, the first convoy set out from Port Sudan two days later, with John Wynn himself frequently taking a turn at driving one of the Contractors. The convoy was accompanied by Bedford fuel tankers provided by Kenana for part of the journey, whilst drinking water was obtained from local wells, often being brought to the convoy by donkey!

At the time, the road between Port Sudan and Khartoum, the capital of Sudan, was still

One of the complete convoys photographed in a scene of utter desolation. It should be obvious form this shot why the convoys had to be self-sufficient.

Apparently, Bedford were so pleased with their involvement in the project and the way that the trucks performed that they featured this photograph in a series of trade advertisements with the copy line 'Desolation Road'!

Tanks were fitted to the swan neck of the step-frame trailers to carry additional fuel and water... drinking water was often delivered to the convoys at rest stops by local donkey!

under construction but even allowing for this, the going was never easy. Whilst there were tarmac sections, the mixture of mountain and desert terrain was a challenge for both men and machines and the trucks were also occasionally required to ford rivers where there were no proper crossing facilities. It was also common to come across overturned local trucks on the highway sections where the Sudanese drivers had fallen asleep at the wheel, or where mechanical failure had caused a runaway accident.

However, the Caterpillar grader more than proved its worth, despite Kenana's oversight in not providing a driver.... an omission ably rectified by Wynns' Peter Milne, and a nice little extra source of income for the company. The huge six-wheeled machine was frequently called upon to drag the loaded trucks out of the soft sand or up steep inclines, and, with plenty of off-road sections to negotiate, the 16ft blade was more than capable of a little on-the-spot road making, on one occasion even building an impromptu railway crossing.

The first convoy arrived at its destination five weeks later, on 19 December having averaged a little under 40 miles a day. Whilst this might seem like slow progress, remember, the heat of the day meant that operations had to cease in early afternoon when the temperature could reach 110oF.

Always reluctant to run empty, on the return journey John actually managed to find a couple of Ruston-Bucyrus 22RB crawler cranes to drag back to Khartoum on behalf of Alfred McAlpine... they had been in use during the construction phase at the Kenana site but, with their tasks completed, had become surplus to requirements.

CONVOYS

The convoys continued until the last load was delivered to Rabak on 10 May 1978. Despite the heat and dust, all of the vehicles acquitted themselves extremely well. The Wynns crews had come to expect reliability from the mighty Scammells, but the TM 6x4s also performed so well that the manufacturers featured the project in

contemporary Bedford advertising.

The Kenana Sugar Company continues in business to this day, claiming to be the 'world's largest integrated sugar company'. The Kenana estate covers 84,078 acres and the factory is designed to process 17,000 tons of sugar cane daily, producing around 330,000 tons of white sugar a year aimed, essentially, at export markets... a tribute to the expertise of the Wynns team and the products of Scammell and Bedford. The company has also diversified in recent years and other products include

animal feeds, molasses, dairy products, timber, woodchips and paper pulp, and agricultural tools and equipment.

This was not the end of Wynns' involvement in Sudan. There was a period when the trucks were contracted to undertake some local spot work, but - as we shall see in the next chapter - the expertise which the company had shown in completing the Kenana run soon led to involvement in a new contract from Polytra NV of Belgium.

John Wynn

Born in October 1932, John Wynn was the son of George ('OG') Wynn and great-grandson to Thomas Wynn who, in 1863, had founded the company.

Seconded for a period to Fairfields at Chepstow, John had trained as a draftsman, his skills being vital in helping to prepare drawings for the Ministry when applying for licences to move unusual loads. He was also apprenticed in engineering with Barings at Cardiff, but his first love was driving. It is fortunate that John was taken under the wing by his Uncle Percy ('HP') Wynn, for this saved him from a life of tedium on the administrative side and allowed him to be a part of the 'sharp end' of the business. There is little doubt that during his working life John acquired unsurpassable knowledge and hands-on experience of moving abnormal loads.

John was heavily involved in the various Sudan contracts. At age 45, after almost 30 years with the company, he had flown out to Sudan to survey the route along which the equipment for the Kenana sugar refinery would be moved. He had quoted for the job and overseen the selection and modification of the vehicles and equipment required. John was with the first convoy which set

out in November 1977 and remained a vital part of the project until the last convoy arrived at Rabak in May 1978. He stayed in Sudan during the months which followed, finding more work for those splendid Scammell Contractors and for the Wynns crews whose expertise moved extraordinary loads across the most difficult terrain.

Along with his cousin Noel, John had been promoted to the board of Wynns in 1960. He stayed with the business following the sale to United Transport in 1964 until the recession of the early 'eighties saw Wynns merged with Sunters under the name United Heavy Transport. In June 1982, after 34 years with the company which his great-grandfather had founded, John resigned... he was irritated by what he saw as management inertia and increasing red tape but, in the end it was the company's refusal to allocate funds for the overhaul of equipment which actually 'broke the camel's back'.

John was never to escape the reputation for moving heavy loads which he had helped Wynns to acquire and, through a lifetime's involvement with heavy haulage, which continues to this day, John has become something of a legend among transport enthusiasts.

WHO DARES WYNNS! PART EIGHT

Conditions in the Sudan were often far from ideal!

...AND STILL IN SUDAN

Continuing from the previous chapter, John Wynn and Pat Ware describe two more contracts which the company undertook in the desert in the late 1970s

These Caterpillar D7 'dozers were amongst the local 'spot' work undertaken following the end of the Kenana contract. The 'dozers were moved from Port Sudan to Khartoum for Seleit Food Production Limited. John Wynn (right) poses with his son Peter.

Previously, we looked at the Kenana Sugar Company project which saw Wynns shift 3000 tons of equipment and supplies across 1000 miles of Sudanese mountain and desert terrain. This was not Wynns first foray into Africa, although it was the first time the company had worked in the challenging conditions which prevailed in Sudan. The completion of the last leg of the project came in May 1978 but this did not spell the end of Wynns involvement in this part of the continent. Immediately after the end of the Kenana contract, there was a period when the trucks undertook some local 'spot' work, involving boats, brewing vats and bulldozers. However, the expertise which the company had shown in completing the Kenana run soon led to involvement in a new project.

Polytra NV, a Belgian transport engineering and logistics company, was the lead transport contractor involved in the construction of the state-owned Sudan-Ren fertiliser plant at Khartoum. Wynns were asked by Polytra to help shift over-sized equipment to the plant, including five huge cylindrical storage vessels and a pair of massive Borsig corner-tube boilers.

More trucks, trailers and equipment were shipped to Sudan for the project. With the addition of the 240-ton

Additional trucks and equipment were shipped to Sudan for the Polytra contract including a Ford tractor and a couple of trailers, one of which was an ex-Ministry tank transporter trailer. Note the jib sections for the Lima crane.

Contractor 'Talisman' (fleet number 196) equipped as a ballast tractor, and 150-ton Contractors 'Traveller' (183), 'Adventurer' (185) and the un-named 280 converted to fifth-wheel configuration, there was a period when Wynns were operating nine Contractors in Africa… almost certainly the largest fleet of Scammells on the continent. Additional trailers included a couple of ex-military Cranes FV3601 50-ton multi-axle tank-transporter units, which proved useful in shifting a huge Caterpillar D8 'dozer, as well as a pair of Cranes four-axle flat-top trailers which could be linked together to provide an eight-axle unit.

Of the smaller trucks which had been purchased for the Kenana project, one of the Bedford TMs, which was effectively worn out, was sold locally and replaced by a 6x4 Atkinson Venturer. A second-hand Lima motorised crane was purchased from Southern Counties of Portsmouth, and refurbished in Wynns' Newport workshops before being shipped to Sudan to assist in loading and unloading the heavy equipment. A small Fordson agricultural tractor was also acquired for use as a shunter, and Sudan-Ren provided a 120-ton Coles motorised crane which was intended for off-loading at the construction site but which also accompanied one of the convoys but which was out of its depth on the rough terrain… the condition of the roads meant that the crane frequently needed 'helping out'.

SUGAR CONTRACT

During the Kenana Sugar contract, the highway between Port Sudan and Khartoum was still under construction and the Wynns convoys were frequently slowed by the difficulty of the terrain. By the time the subsequent convoys got underway, more of the highway had been completed which meant that there were fewer off-road excursions. In fact, despite being able to employ a hydraulically-suspended trailer which allowed the load to be maintained on a level keel, John Wynn reports that it would have been impossible to deliver the enormous corner-tube boilers without the completion of the metalled road.

One of the most demanding loads of the contract was the corner tube boilers, each of which weighed in at 83 tons and measured 27 feet in height. Carried on a Cranes eight-axle flat-top trailer, the boilers towered above the tractor, whilst the offset centre of gravity meant that the load was hanging off one side of the trailer by four feet. Tom Davies took the wheel of 'Talisman' and John Dixon rode shotgun for the entire run, controlling the hydraulics which kept the load upright across some very difficult road conditions, including extreme cambers… this was no small feat and required absolute concentration for mile after mile. The height of the load caused particular problems in the city of Khartoum, where overhead cables had to be raised to allow the boiler to pass underneath. Equally challenging in their own way were the five 85-ton bullet storage vessels, 120-foot long and 11 feet in diameter. Each was carried on the same type of Cranes trailer as the boilers, but this time running as a pair of separate four-axle bogie bolster sets.

Although the Scammells proved themselves exceptionally reliable, the extreme heat and dust of the Sudan quickly began to take its toll on their appearance and after a few months exposure the once resplendent gleaming red paint was faded and scuffed.

More 'spot' work was also undertaken in Sudan during the Sudan-Ren contract. Loads handled during this time included a pair of RB22 excavators, a truck-mounted crane, a JCB excavator, two 75-ton dockside cranes which were moved half a mile within the Port Sudan docks… and, most notably, a 75-ton NCK crawler crane which was moved 725 miles from Port Sudan to Burri Power Station at Khartoum for machinery erectors Capper Neil International. Although the crane was generally carried on one trailer, with the jib and other components on another, for at least one part of the journey the load was hauled, road-train style, on a pair of trailers coupled together and headed by a single Scammell 240-ton tractor… as the company themselves used to say, 'There's a Scammell for every type of load'… and indeed there is!

MASSIVE CONVOY

No sooner was the Sudan-Ren project out of the way than Polytra asked Wynns to join a massive convoy which was

The 83-ton corner tube boilers were over-height and over-width… and the centre of gravity was heavily offset to one side.

The vehicles moved in convoys, thus ensuring that help was always at hand in the event of mechanical breakdown or off-road excursions.

John Dixon rode shotgun on the boiler trailer for the entire Kenana project, controlling the hydraulics which kept the load upright. This was no small feat and required absolute concentration for mile after mile, not easy when tucked away at the back of the trailer.

Another 'spot' hire contract saw these dockside cranes moved half a mile within the docks at Port Sudan. 'Talisman' proves more than equal to the task.

transporting equipment to a huge factory site in Nyala, the largest city in South Darfur and deep in the oil-rich west of the country. The work was being carried out for Held & Francke, a German company which was undertaking groundworks and constructing roadways at the complex.

This project saw Wynns providing Scammell Contractors 'Conqueror' and 'Hercules' (183, 192) as part of a massive 50-vehicle one-off convoy hauling trucks, dumpers and other plant and equipment southwest of Khartoum and south of the Darfur region. Although there was a rail link between the two cities it was not suitable for moving the heavy and out-of-

gauge loads in question and since there was no proper road, the convoy ran on little more than tracks across 400 miles of desert and distinctive African scrubland.

The Wynns trucks were accompanied by the Bedford KM 'chuck wagon' which had already done sterling service on the Sudan-Ren contract, and a Land Rover. Wynns' contribution to the exercise was to carry two massive Broyt hydraulic shovels, one older X4 and one X41, loaded on three-axle step-frame semi-trailers and coupled to a pair of 240-ton Contractors. For their part, Helde & Francke deployed a fleet of MAN 6x4 tankers, tractors and tippers, the latter often hauling trailers,

which were carrying rock-crushing plant, spare tyres for the wheeled equipment, and the smaller items of plant. Running under their own power, the convoy also included a fleet of brand-new Euclid scow-ended dump trucks.

ATROCIOUS ROUTE

For most of the route the going was atrocious, with obstacles such as soft sand, narrow bridges, and dry gulleys. It was also frequently necessary to unload one of the Caterpillar 'dozers or graders being carried by one of the other contractors to help extricate trucks, including Wynns' Contractors, which had become bogged down in the sand. Worse still, the heat was such that it was only possible to travel from first light until early afternoon before the daytime heat became unbearable.

Although other commitments forced him to return to the UK before the contract was completed, John Wynn was a vital member of the convoy crew, taking a hand at driving and the inevitable digging out, as well as

'Hercules' and 'Conqueror' struggle through the Sudan thicket during the Polytra run to Nyala.

Tommy Cromwell (jnr) watches carefully as 'Conqueror' negotiates a narrow humped-back bridge. The paint is beginning to look very worn after months under the African sun.

Adventurer' remained in Sudan at the end of the Polytra contract and was scrapped.

Loaded with a Broyt X41 shovel loader, 'Conqueror' raises the Sudanese dust.

The corner boilers made a fine spectacle on the streets of Khartoum.

acting as banksman as the outfits picked their way through narrow ravines and gulleys. Wynns' veteran Tommy Cromwell also retired at the end of the Nyala project, after a lifetime with the company.

Of the trucks used on the project, most were disposed of locally, including the Atkinson and the Scammell Contractors 'Conqueror' (182), 'Traveller' (183), and the un-named 280; 'Adventurer' (185), dating from 1967, also remained in the Sudan and was scrapped when the contract was over.

In June 1982, frustrated with poor management decisions and the increasing climate of red tape, John Wynn resigned from the board of Wynns' Heavy Haulage. His 34-year career with the company had spanned his entire working life and at the time it must have seemed like the world had come to an end... but, 'never say never again' for by the end of the year he was back in Sudan moving oversized loads... this time at the wheel of a Scammell Super Constructor in the livery of Transport & Handling International Enterprise of Port Sudan. ▪

John Wynn

Born in October 1932, John Wynn was the son of George ('OG') Wynn and great-grandson to Thomas Wynn who, in 1863, had founded the company.

Initially destined for an office job, John was seconded for a period to Fairfields at Chepstow, where he trained as a draughtsman, and was also apprenticed in engineering with Bearings at Cardiff. His drawing office skills proved vital in helping to prepare drawings for the Ministry giving axle spacings and weights which were required when applying for permits to move unusual loads on the road. By studying engineering, he was also following in the footsteps of Uncle Percy ('HP') Wynn who was responsible for many of the practical innovations in trailer design and load handling which kept Wynns at the top of the industry.

But John's first love was driving and when he was taken under the wing by 'HP', he was saved from what could have been a life of tedium on the administrative side. Through his involvement in the 'sharp end' of the

business John acquired unsurpassable knowledge and hands-on experience of moving abnormal loads.

When he eventually inherited what had been Percy's role in the company, it was inevitable that John would become heavily involved in all significant new projects. As we saw previously, at age 45, after almost 30 years with the company, he had flown out to Sudan to survey the route along which the equipment for the Kenana sugar refinery would be moved... he had also quoted for the job and planned the vehicle and logistical requirements.

FIRST CONVOY

John travelled with the first convoy and remained a vital part of the project until the last convoy arrived at Rabak in May 1978. During the months which followed, John found the spot work which kept the trucks and crews busy until the Polytra contract.

John, and his cousin Noel, had been promoted to the board of Wynns in 1960 and stayed with the business following the sale to United Transport in 1964 and into the recession of the early 'eighties when Wynns merged

with Sunters under the name United Heavy Transport. At this point, although John remained with the business - at least for a while - Noel opted for early retirement.

After his formal retirement, Noel went on to become chairman of the Road Haulage Association (RHA), county chairman of the Confederation of British Industry (CBI), member of the national and Wales councils of the CBI, and a fellow of the Chartered Institute of Logistics and Transport (CILT). Noel passed away, aged 87, on 12 May 2008.

In June 1982, after 34 years with the company which his great-grandfather had founded, John tendered his resignation. The decision was brought about by what John saw as management inertia and increasing red tape, as well as the company's refusal to allocate funds for the overhaul of equipment.

John was never to escape the reputation for moving heavy loads which he had helped Wynns to acquire and, through a lifetime's involvement with heavy haulage, which continues to this day, John has become something of a legend among transport enthusiasts.

WHO DARES WYNNS!
PART NINE

Everything stops for tea!

ON THE ROAD AGAIN

Although he had resigned from Wynns, John Wynn was soon back in Sudan with a new company. With help from Pat Ware, he describes his relationship with Enescon and THIE and chronicles the demise of the family firm

The two tractors and the condenser were forced to wait at the bottom of the Aqaba Pass for the traffic coming down to be halted.

In 1982, John returned from the Sudan and told the directors of British Electric Traction, who by this time had taken over United Transport (which, you will remember, had bought Wynns back in the early 1960s) that there was a third big Sudan contract in the offing, but it

would require investment of some £75,000 to refurbish and overhaul the tractors and equipment which had already seen such hard service in Sudan. "Do you have the signed contract?" he was asked. He replied that "things weren't always done that way in the Wynns world", but was

informed that, in which case, there would be no money because that was how things were done by BET.

As far as John was concerned, this was the last straw in a sorry saga of mismanagement and excessive red tape. Adopting the only course that seemed available to him, he resigned,

John and Tag sign the contract that made John a director of THIE.

Ex-Wynns trailer number 456, as bought from Hardwicks, at Ewell.

The first move that John undertook in his new role involved this large launch, Juliet Sarah, which was moved from Port Sudan to Khartoum, a distance of about 800 miles.

This turnbuckle was the method adopted to keep the bolster locking pin in place to prevent the trailer from wandering out of line. Admittedly it was a bit of a jury rig – but it worked.

this particular conversation, he learned that Tag had already quoted for the job, but believed that the magic of the name Wynn would swing it for him. Seemingly with nothing to lose, John agreed and, meeting Tag at an hotel in Newbury, signed an agreement that made him a director of Transport & Handling International Enterprise (THIE), Enescon's local transport company. And indeed, this was sufficient to ensure that THIE was awarded the NEI contract.

Returning to the Sudan, John was told that THIE already owned a near-

an action that ultimately annoyed the Wynns' management so much that they refused to cooperate with him in the months to come, even where it would have been in the interests of both parties. At the same time, his cousin Noel elected to take early retirement, almost signalling the end of the involvement of the Wynn family in the business that still bore their name. John's son, Peter, hung on for another two years or so but, by 1983, the name of Wynns had vanished from the vehicles altogether.

John believed that he now faced possible unemployment, something which he had never previously contemplated. But no sooner had word got out that John Wynn was no longer employed by Wynns than Tageldean Elkhazin – known to everyone simply as Tag – the proprietor of Enescon, got in touch with him and insisted that, with John's help, Tag could secure the contract to shift two condensers for the British company NEI from the docks at Port Sudan to a new power station that was being constructed in Khartoum. This was the very contract for which John had been trying to obtain investment from the directors of BET. John had originally got to know Tag during his previous forays in Sudan and, during the course of

As supplied, the Super Constructor was equipped with a fifth wheel for work with semi-trailers.

A ballast box was fabricated for the Super Constructor by using 10 feet cut from the rear end of ex-Wynns trailer number 328 – a Dyson unit.

It wasn't very pretty, but it got the job done. The photograph was taken on 9 January, 1983.

The Glory Days of Heavy Haulage

new Rolls-Royce C6SL-engined Scammell Super Constructor – the last one that Scammell ever built – as well as a couple of Crusaders. The Constructor was equipped as a fifth-wheel tractor and had been used for various local heavy haulage jobs. THIE had also bought two brand-new bonneted Scammell S24 tractors – neither of which, it seems, was ever paid for. The trucks were painted yellow with white roofs – to offset the heat of the sun – and proudly displayed the THIE logo on the doors, now including the legend "with John Wynn".

The company also owned a couple of ex-Wynns trailers of which BET had seen fit to dispose. However, it was clear that if THIE was to undertake any serious heavy haulage work then a hydraulic steering trailer would be required. Quite by coincidence, Hardwicks at Ewell – now long gone, but in its day a well-known yard to all fans of surplus machinery – had ex-Wynns trailer 456 for sale, an eight-axle double swan-neck unit. The trailer had originally been bought by HP (Percy Wynn), from Cranes, back in September, 1960, at a cost of £22,500. It was, to say the least, well used.

MUCH AMUSED

THIE bought 456 from Hardwicks without John actually knowing which trailer it was before it arrived in Sudan. At the time, Wynns were still at work in Sudan moving four 240-ton diesel engines from Port Sudan to Khartoum for a power station project being constructed by Capper Neil and John agreed to meet with Wynns' John Dixon who said he had mail for him.

Colin Kilby surveys the rig and wonders what he has let himself in for.

Dixon was much amused as he told John Wynn that the trailer was number 456 and he agreed, against company orders but in a spirit of friendship and loyalty to John, that Wynns' crew would offload the trailer from the ship and move it to THIE's yard at Port Sudan. The first job undertaken by John during his time with THIE, and one which he did completely on his own, involved moving a large launch, Juliet Sarah, from Port Sudan to Khartoum, a distance of about 800 miles. The cab of the Crusader tractor was comparatively cramped and it was a lonely job, but at least on the outward journey the launch gave John somewhere a little more spacious to sleep during overnight stops.

Meanwhile, the S24s had been shipped to Port Sudan, where the inevitable paperwork delays at the docks meant that they sat on the dockside for a month or more. John was becoming increasingly impatient to get started on the NEI project and when word finally came that the trucks could be released, he asked his new partners where the keys could be found. "At the dock office," was the reply, so John went down there with a couple of drivers, finding the tractors hidden behind a wall of mealie (maize) sacks. Once again, John asked about the keys and was astonished when the man from the dock office took him outside and counted-off so many sacks from one end of the wall, before sticking his hand in between a couple of them. Triumphantly, he produced the keys. It's difficult to imagine what on earth would have happened had the sacks been shipped out or had the dock manager fallen off the jetty or moved on.

Back at the THIE yard, it had

It's 28 January, 1983 and the rig is finally on the move – at the moment, without the Wynns' tractor.

The Glory Days of Heavy Haulage

Once the Aqaba Pass had been negotiated, the S24 completed the condenser move without the assistance of the Wynns tractor.

become apparent that the choice of a fifth-wheel tractor meant that the Super Constructor was restricted to hauling semi-trailers and so, in December 1982, the decision was taken to build a ballast body to fit across the chassis over the fifth-wheel. The body was constructed locally by effectively cannibalising the last 10 feet of ex-Wynns trailer 328, a Dyson unit which by that time was redundant. Colin Betteress, an engineer from Scammell, had popped over to Sudan from Saudi to see how the team was getting on with the new trucks and was persuaded to help with the conversion project. When completed, this gave the best of both worlds, allowing the tractor to be readily converted from one configuration to the other, which increased its versatility. Now THEI was equipped with a pair of Scammell S24s, a ballast-bodied Super Constructor and a hydraulic trailer, so all that was needed was a hydraulics man to steer the thing. John knew just the man and ex-Wynns steersman Colin Kilby was persuaded to join the team in the Sudan.

Everything was now in place to

move the two 76-ton condensers, which had been delivered to Port Sudan in January, 1983. At the docks, the first condenser was loaded on to the trailer and the crew ran the outfit around the dock roads to check the steering and brakes. They were not impressed. It was a 32-wheeled trailer, but John recalls that they never could persuade the brakes on more than 16 of the wheels to operate. Nevertheless,

this was the trailer on which they moved the two 76-ton condensers across Sudan. Clearly, the Sudanese authorities took a fairly relaxed view of such matters.

While the Super Constructor was plenty powerful, John took the view that two tractors would be required to get the load up the Aqaba Pass (the word is Arabic for 'difficult'), some 10 miles outside Port Sudan. He elected to approach Wynns who, at the time, were still working on the Capper Neil project. Peter Sunter, who had taken over the management of the Capper Neil job when John quit, had persuaded the Sudanese that three more tractors were required, together with what John describes as "more wheels". Permission had already been obtained to use a 20-line flat-top, but Sunter, anxious to make his own mark and perhaps increase the profitability of the job, changed the specification of the job to use four sets of seven wheels. All of this equipment was still in the country and, believing that a Wynns Contractor would be just the job to provide the additional power that he needed, John Wynn asked John Dixon for assistance. It seems that

The second condenser was moved without the Wynns Contractor and John elected to ballast a semi-trailer and use one of the S24s to provide additional power.

John poses in front of the rig. The auxiliary fuel tank can be seen on top of the ballast in the Scammell's home-made ballast box.

Dixon had been instructed not to assist John without prior approval from the UK and, although this approval was eventually granted, it came at a price.

IMPRESSIVE CONVOY

Wynns agreed to provide one of their Contractors for half a day at a (1983) price of £900, rather than the £150-£200 that might have been charged in the UK. They say that what goes around comes around, and this meanness of spirit had its consequences. Once word got back to the UK about how Wynns had treated John, and the consequent risks to the project, NEI refused to give Wynns, the company, any more work.

Meanwhile, on 27 January, 1983, Wynns completed the Capper Neil project, meaning that the Contractor was available. The next day, the two big Scammells rolled out of Port Sudan ready for the climb up the Aqaba Pass. The Super Constructor was ballasted with big concrete blocks, on top of which had been chained a 1,000-gallon fuel tank. The weight of this also helped provide traction for the rear wheels. At the pass, a police officer was despatched to the top of the incline to hold back oncoming traffic, asking the driver of the last vehicle going down to tell the convoy that it could start its ascent.

Using second and third gear, the impressive convoy began the long, three-hour climb, reaching the top at 14.00 hours. The team paused for a well-deserved break and, with its work completed, the Wynns Contractor returned to Port Sudan.

THIE undertook other heavy haulage jobs in this period and here we see one of the Crusader tractors with a load of Canadian agricultural equipment. The local driver, Sim Sim, drove for 10 days across 130 miles of desert with this rig.

For the rest of the run, the Super Constructor took the load on its own. There were problems with the hydraulics on the trailer, which slowed the convoy down, but the load arrived at Khartoum at 10.15 on 2 February, six days after setting out.

John now turned his thoughts to the second condenser, having already decided that he would make the move without the Wynns Contractor. He loaded 25 tons of ballast into a semi-trailer coupled to the S24 and used this, together with the Super Constructor, to provide the power required. The local man who was driving the S24 was told to stay in first gear up the pass, as did John, driving the Super Constructor. It worked and they completed the climb, but John says that the gear ratios of the two trucks were badly mismatched, and during the long climb up the pass he became very conscious of the lack of big company back-up and started to wonder whether he had done the right thing in leaving Wynns. But things have a way of working out for the best. Other projects were in the offing in other corners of the globe.

FAMILY FORTUNES

John Wynn was born in October, 1932, the son of George 'OG' Wynn and great-grandson to Thomas Wynn who, in 1863, founded the company. From an early age, John spent much of his spare time at the company yard and it soon became clear that his first love was driving. Each of the older Wynn brothers had an area of expertise. John's father, OG, was responsible for the administration of the business, which didn't interest John at all so it is fortunate that, from the age of 16, he was taken under the wing by his Uncle Percy 'HP' Wynn. Percy's patronage saved John from what he believed would be a life of tedium in the office and allowed him to be part of the sharp end of the business. Frequently acting as Percy's driver, he was presented with the perfect opportunity of picking the older man's brains during the long hours they spent together in the car.

There is little doubt that John was able to acquire unsurpassable knowledge and hands-on experience of moving abnormal loads during his years with the company. Along with his cousin, Noel, John was voted to the board of Wynns in 1960. Both stayed with the business following the sale to United Transport in 1964. Since 1956, some 20 per cent of United Transport had been owned by the large British industrial conglomerate known initially as the British Electric Traction Company, but subsequently renamed BET plc in 1985. BET increased their stake in United Transport to 100 per cent in 1971, which meant that they now effectively owned United Transport and thus also owned Wynns, Wrekin Roadways and Sunters, of Northallerton. Both Sunters and Wrekin Roadways had originally been competitors to Wynns, but the recession of the early 1980s saw them both merged with Wynns under the name United Heavy Transport. John hated the big business ethos of BET and his increasing frustrations with the company's management style led to his resignation in June, 1982, after 34 years with the company that his great-grandfather had founded. However, on the basis that a man cannot evade his destiny, John never did escape the reputation for moving heavy loads that he had helped Wynns acquire.

It is ironic, perhaps, that although BET retained the transport business of United Transport for the next decade, the company was acquired by Rentokil in a hostile takeover bid in 1996. Now trading as Rentokil Initial, the company has no transport interests, aside from offering courier services. On the other hand, the Wynn family is back in heavy haulage through John's son, Peter – but more of that anon. Through a lifetime's involvement with heavy haulage, which continues to this day, John has become something of a legend among transport enthusiasts.

ANTAR EAT

The post-war Rotinoff Atlantic was a brave attempt by an independent company to produce a heavy tractor suitable for tank transporter duties and could have given the Antar a run for its money. Pat Ware has the story

Above: Although it was said to be available in both ballast tractor and fifth wheel form, most photographs show the ballast tractor. This Super Atlantic is hitched to the British FV3601 50-ton multi-wheeled trailer.

In the annals of super trucks, the Rotinoff is something of a legend. The brainchild of George A Rotinoff, a White Russian immigrant who had come to the UK at the age of two, the Rolls-Royce-powered Atlantic GR7 first appeared in the mid-fifties and was marketed for use as a tank transporter or heavy haulage tractor. Later models included the Super Atlantic, suitable for gross train weights up to 200 tons, and the smaller Viscount, intended for Australian road-train operation.

Rotinoff had started his post-war career converting Sherman tanks into bulldozers, by little more than removing the turret and fitting a winch-controlled 'dozer blade. By 1952, the company, which was based in the village of Poyle near Slough, had started work on the design of a heavy tractor for tank-transporter duties.

The first production example appeared in 1955, and was known as the Atlantic GR7. Rated for a gross train weight of 140 tons, the GR7 was a heavy-duty 6x4 tractor powered by a Rolls-Royce C6SFL six-cylinder supercharged diesel engine, producing 250bhp from 12.17 litres, and driving Kirkstall axles at the rear through a 12-speed David Brown transmission (4F1Rx3). All-wheel drive and automatic transmission were offered as an option. Later models used the turbocharged C6TFL version of this engine, together with a 15-speed transmission. Hydraulic power steering was fitted as standard, requiring just 4.5 turns from lock to lock, and suspension was by multi-leaf semi-elliptical springs, inverted at the rear. The rear axles incorporated double-reduction gearing, using worm gears for the primary reduction and what was described as 'patented epicyclic gears' for the secondary reduction; ball-ended radius arms were used to take the slewing and braking loads. Wheels

were 24in diameter at the front and 25in at the rear, and the buyer could also choose either 14.00-24 twin rear tyres or 18.00-25 singles. The main chassis members were a massive 12.675in (322mm) deep and were pressed from 0.5in (12.7mm) thick steel; the three-man all-steel cab was of twin-skin insulated construction and featured sliding doors, and the ballast tractor incorporated a welded steel body incorporating equipment lockers.

A 50,000 lb mechanical winch was mounted behind the cab and was driven via a power take-off on the gearbox; fairlead rollers were provided front and rear.

Although most surviving photographs show the tractor in ballast body form –

'This was the first vehicle to exceed a train weight of 200 tons on British roads.'

usually coupled to a British FV3601 50-ton multi-wheeled trailer – the tractor could also be supplied fitted with a standardised fifth wheel for use with a semi-trailer.

With its long bonnet and no-nonsense engineering, it was an impressive vehicle, in a similar mould to the WW2 Diamond T Model 980/981 and the Thornycroft Antar, both of which were in use by the British Army at that time.

The similar, but more powerful, Super Atlantic GR7 appeared in 1957 and was also offered as a ballast or fifth-wheel tractor. An eight-cylinder C8TFL turbocharged engine, producing 366bhp from 16.2 litres, replaced the six-cylinder Rolls-Royce C Series unit. The uprated truck was said to be capable of operating at a gross train weight of up to 200 tons, depending on statutory limitations. It was equally suitable for use as a high-speed tank transporter and was capable of 40mph (65km/h) on the road. The standard transmission was a manual five-speed main gearbox in conjunction with a three-speed auxiliary 'box, giving a total of 15 gears, but automatic transmission was available as an option, as was all-wheel drive. The rear bogie was of the double-reduction type like that fitted to the Atlantic, but a third, lockable, differential was incorporated in the foremost axle.

An Atlantic tractor was trialled by the British War Office in 1955. Despite the use of a diesel engine - which the War Office considered highly desirable, but

ER?

Above: Surprisingly, the Atlantic fitted nicely into the Atkinson truck range alongside the 6x6 Omega heavy-duty tractor which Atkinson had introduced in 1960. This Omega is coupled to an FV3541 30-ton low-loading trailer, and is being put through its paces at FVRDE's Chertsey test track.

In all its glory... the Rotinoff Super Atlantic. This preserved example appears regularly at the Great Dorset Steam Fair. (Paul Sharpe)

When Atkinson took over the design in 1962, they seem to have made no changes beyond attaching their 'circle A' badge to the radiator. Both the Atlantic and the heavier Super Atlantic were described in this 1963 sales brochure.

which did not appear in the Antar until the Mk 3 appeared in 1958 - it seems that the Rotinoff was not able to offer sufficient advantage over the Antar to replace it, and there were no volume purchases. However, the Swiss Army, which had run comparative trials between the Atlantic and Antar, opted for the former, placing an order for ten ballast tractors for use with a 50-ton Scheuerle trailer on which it placed its Centurion tanks. By the time the first examples were delivered in 1958, the Super Atlantic had been developed and the remaining seven were supplied in the more powerful guise. In

1957, the British heavy haulage company, Sunters, purchased one example of the Atlantic fitted with a crew cab, and this was the first vehicle to exceed a train weight of 200 tons on British roads; 18 tractors were also supplied to the Iraqi Army and there is some suggestion that the South African Army had one.

The smaller Viscount was developed during 1955/56 and, although it was also trialled by the British Army, was intended for use on Australian road-train duties, hauling multiple trailers across the country's vast interior. Three versions were offered - the GR37, which was fitted with a Rolls-Royce diesel engine, the

GR64 which was powered by a Rolls-Royce B81 petrol engine, and the forward-control GKS64.

George Rotinoff died of a heart attack on 2 May 1959 at the age of just 55 and, a year later, the company name was changed to Lomount. In 1962, the model range was taken over by Atkinson Vehicles of Preston, which continued to market the machines under the names Atlantic and Super Atlantic for another year or so, alongside its own 6x6 Omega heavy-duty cross-country tractor – which was also trialled as a tank transporter!

Total production is said to have amounted to just 35 vehicles, but a further 15 examples may have been constructed under the names Lomount and/or Atkinson; 11 vehicles are said to still exist, at least four of which are in the UK... oh yes, and there was also a Matchbox toy!

THE BRONTOSA

Geoff Fletcher investigates the fate of Leyland's one-off FV1000

In 1946, the War Office began to plan for a new range of military vehicles. The range was to consist of off-the-shelf commercial (CL) vehicles, general service (GS) vehicles based on modified commercial chassis, and combat (CT) vehicles built to meet the military's specific needs. In this latter category were to fall a variety of types ranging from the 1/4-ton Austin Champ FV1800 to the largest of all, the Leyland 60-ton 6x6 FV1000. Several of the CT category vehicles fell by the wayside, although a number did enter service - for instance the Austin Champ FV1800, Humber 1-ton FV1600, and Leyland Martian 6x6 FV1100. However, this feature is about the largest of all the CT trucks... known as the Leyland Brontosaurus, and only one was ever made.

There were intended to be three versions of the FV1000: a ballast body tractor, for towing a full-trailer (FV1001); a fifth wheel tractor, for towing a tank transporter semi-trailer (FV1003); and a heavy recovery vehicle (FV1004). In practice, only one vehicle was built, a tank transporter, intended (with the aid of a special FV3300 semi-trailer) to tow the mighty 65-ton Conqueror tank. It was given the civilian registration LYN 60.

The vehicle was supposed to be powered by a huge diesel engine, but none was available, so the 498bhp Rover Meteorite engine was installed instead. The project got underway in 1947 and the vehicle was delivered to Chertsey for trials in 1950. If you want the full story of the tractor you should read the relevant pages of Pat Ware's *Tugs of War*. In a nutshell, however, the requirement to transport Conquerors was solved more economically by using the commercially developed Thornycroft Antar and, in March 1955, it was announced that the FV1000 project had been dropped.

My recent interest in this vehicle began when a contact sent me a photograph taken by Dave Stretton at Heanor Haulage's yard in Nottingham. It showed what he described as a Leyland Brontosaurus tractor, dimly lit, but clearly with forward control. On the front bumper is the number '1019', which I recognised as a lot number from the Ruddington auction sales of surplus government vehicles that were held from

RUS

just after WW2 until 1982. However, although the tractor looked similar in size to FV1000, it was forward control, whereas the original FV1000 was normal control. Pat Ware confirmed that it looked like FV1000 as it had the same wheel arch shapes, but could add little to what had already appeared in *Tugs of War*.

There the story might have rested, but whilst working my way through some of Bovington Tank Museum's huge collection, I found some photographs of the same vehicle loaded on a Leyland Crusader and semi-trailer. These photographs were taken at the Military Vehicle Experimental Establishment (MVEE) Chertsey in about September 1976, and are part of their own photographic collection. This then led me to look at the Ruddington auction catalogues after that date.

My search of the catalogues was quickly over. Only the second one I looked at after September 1976 (for the 144th sale that ran from

14-16 December 1976) had a lot described as a Leyland Brontosaurus. What is more, the registration is shown as LYN 60 and it was described as a 'gradient simulation vehicle', which is exactly how Pat described its fate in *Tugs of War!*

So the photographs I had found at Bovington show the vehicle in its final state and were presumably taken as it was loaded for its journey from Chertsey to

Ruddington to await sale. All those pipes and boxes on the back were added to 'simulate gradients', and the vehicle was converted to forward control to provide a bigger platform for them. The only question left is... how do you simulate gradients?

The accompanying photos, courtesy of Bovington Tank Museum, show the Leyland FV1000 Brontosaurus in its final form as a 'gradient simulation vehicle'. It is being carried on a 35-tonne semi-trailer, towed by a Leyland Crusader tractor.

The semi-trailer was permanently attached to the tractor and was loaded via the removable rear bogie. (Tank Museum)

MOVING THE TANKS

Pat Ware takes an overview of five generations of British heavy tank transporter... and concludes that the scoreline is UK 3 - USA 2, just giving the edge to the home team!

The French invented the modern tank... by which I mean a tracked armoured vehicle mounting a gun in a revolving turret. And, what's more, there is photographic evidence that the French appear to have also invented the tank transporter... the British being content to move their heavier, tanks either on their tracks or on railway wagons. However, early tanks were notoriously unreliable and it soon became obvious that the more they were used, the more maintenance they required and tank transporters were clearly an essential component of their deployment.

Unlike the French Renault FT17, which was of modest proportions, the larger British tanks could not be carried on flat-bed trucks and the first purpose-designed tank transporter appeared in 1919, consisting of a modified AEC K chassis with a semi-trailer built by H C Bauly and Sons. Sadly, it was too late for the Great War but, anyway, there wasn't much stomach for defence spending at the time and just one example was constructed. It does, at least, carry the distinction of having established the design parameters for tank transporters for

the next 100 years... which is no mean feat... and its spirit certainly lives on through the five generations of British tank transporter.

But, by the late 'thirties, it seemed that Britain faced the prospect of entering the next war, which was surely on the horizon, without a satisfactory tank transporter. OK, some of the smaller tanks of the period could be carried on the backs of flat-bed trucks, but it wasn't until the War Office purchased the Scammell Pioneer

that the Army was in a position to move larger tanks such as the Covenanter and Crusader.

SCAMMELL PIONEER

Work on the six-wheeled Scammell Pioneer had started in 1925 with P C Hugh working under the design direction of the talented Oliver North. The prototype, which appeared a year later, featured enormous balloon tyres and the unique drive-line and suspension system which became almost a trademark of Scammell heavy vehicles for the next 30 years.

The front axle was pivoted at its centre and was suspended on an inverted semi-elliptical multi-leaf spring and located by an A frame attached to a ball-pivot perch on the chassis, allowing considerable movement. A single rear axle was suspended on longitudinal semi-elliptical springs; on each end of the axle there was a walking beam gearcase which allowed the wheels on each side of the vehicle to move by around a foot (300mm) relative to one another in a vertical plane. Because the gearcases were pivoted on the axle ends, the wheels on either side of the vehicle were also able to move independently of one another. It was an excellent arrangement which gave the Pioneer an unprecedented degree of off-road performance for a heavy vehicle.

By 1928/29, Scammell was offering the Pioneer in 6x6 and 6x4 forms and, in 1932, the War Office purchased a single 6x4 example for trials as a tank transporter. Described as 'tractor-trailer, tank transporter', and powered by a Gardner six-cylinder diesel engine, the vehicle was attached to semi-trailer and was intended for use with the Vickers medium tank. Where the Bauly semi-trailer which was hauled by the

In 1932, the War Office purchased a single example of the Scammell Pioneer 6x4 for trials as a tank transporter. (Tank Museum)

The standard Pioneer tank transporter of WW2 had a 30-ton semi-trailer with long folding ramps at the rear. (BCVMT Archives)

Despite being somewhat archaic in appearance, the unique suspension and drive-line and superb Gardner 6LW diesel engine gave the Pioneer a reputation for never giving up, no matter how tough the going. (BCVMT Archives)

AEC was loaded via ramps, the Pioneer had a detachable rear bogie which allowed the rear of the trailer to sit on the ground, effectively making ramps unnecessary. Whilst this might have had some advantages, it was in the days before hydraulics, and it certainly did not speed the loading process.

It remained a one-off and was quickly relegated to training duties.

It was not until 1938 or 1939 that the Army seemed suddenly to realise that perhaps having more than one tank transporter might not be a bad idea. An initial order was placed with Scammell for eight fifth-wheel tractor-trailer outfits rated at 20 tons. The tractor, designated TRMU/20, was powered by Gardner's 6LW diesel engine driving the rear wheels through a six-speed gearbox, whilst the trailer, which was non-detachable, was identified as TRCU/20. As with the original, loading was effected by removing the rear bogie, a laborious business involving the use of screw jacks.

The semi-trailer was swiftly redesigned to incorporate folding ramps which speeded the loading process, and was subsequently redesigned again to raise the capacity from 20 tons to 30 tons, the outfit by this time being described as TRMU/30 + TRCU/30.

this form, some 550 were produced between 1939 and 1945.

DIAMOND T MODEL 980/981
As WW2 ground on, tanks became larger and heavier. Despite experiments with a ballast tractor conversion and draw-bar trailer, it was obvious that the Scammell Pioneer could not be up-rated beyond its 30-ton figure which meant

that it was not suitable for carrying the 40-ton Churchill except in an emergency. Even if further upgrading had been feasible, there was simply no spare production capacity available, since Scammell was also producing artillery tractor and recovery versions of the vehicle.

The War Office was forced to look elsewhere and, in 1940, the Washington-based British Purchasing Commission approached a number of American heavy truck manufacturers including Mack, Ward La France, Diamond T and White. Diamond T was the company selected and, in conjunction with the British authorities, it took a standard heavy-duty truck chassis and, from it, developed a diesel-engined ballast tractor which, coupled with a multi-wheeled draw-bar trailer, was capable of hauling 40-45 tons.

In 1941, the British ordered 485 of these Diamond T tractors but, by the time production had come to an end in 1945, some 5871 examples had been constructed and the truck was used by all of the Allies including the Americans.

The Diamond T was identified by its maker as the Models 980 and 981, with the difference confined to the provision of winch fairlead rollers at the front, and with its original art-deco cab, many still consider this the best-looking truck of all time. It was powered by a six-cylinder Hercules DXFE power plant driving the rear wheels through a four-speed main gearbox and three-speed auxiliary 'box. The original cab was abandoned in 1943 when it was replaced by the semi-standardised open cab which was being specified for all American vehicles, both to save steel and to reduce the overall height.

Aside from the changes to the cab, the design was scarcely modified at all during the War, although a number were converted to fifth-wheel tractors to enable them to be used with similar semi-trailers to those used with the Scammell. And, during the 'fifties, many of those which remained in British Army service had their original Hercules engines replaced by Rolls-Royce C6NFL units.

THORNYCROFT ANTAR
By the end of the War, the British Army still owned 1200 Diamond Ts. Clearly, they were not getting any younger and, equally, were not really up to the task of moving the massive 65-ton Conqueror which was planned to start entering service in the early 'fifties.

There was a brief flirtation with two Leyland-

The original military Thornycroft Antar was a steel-bodied ballast tractor, very much in the same mould as the Diamond T. (Tank Museum)

built heavy tractors - the FV1000 and the FV1200 - though neither made it into production and the slowness of these projects meant that the War Office was faced with taking delivery of a tank for which there no suitable transporter. As it happened, rescue came from an unlikely quarter.

In 1948, in collaboration with Geo Wimpey, Thornycroft had started design work on a massive 6x4 prime mover for the Iraq Petroleum Company. Named Mighty Antar, and billed as the 'largest commercial tractor available in Britain', the vehicle was first shown to the trade press in mid-1950 and was exhibited at the Commercial Motor Show later that same year.

Powered by a 250bhp Meteorite V8 diesel engine, the first commercial Antars were supplied with a skeletal trailer for carrying sections of oil pipeline. The transmission was a complex affair consisting of a four-speed main gearbox and three-speed ancillary box with a fair amount of overlap between the various combinations of gears. Live axles were suspended on semi-elliptical springs and there were air-pressure brakes and power-assisted steering. Lacking the elegance of the Diamond T, the perpendicular cab looked distinctly old-fashioned.

However, the War Office certainly sat up and took considerable notice. Here was a commercial tractor, reputedly rated at 85 tons, which could be bought almost literally 'off the shelf'. It must have seemed almost too good to be true and, in 1951, the Ministry of Supply issued a contract to Thornycroft for 15 Mk 1 Antar tractors (FV12001) with a normally-aspirated Meteorite petrol engine producing 260bhp gross from 18,012cc.

In 1953, a fifth-wheel variant was

produced for use with 50- and 60-ton semi-trailers. Designated Antar Mk 2 (FV12002), this differed only in detail from the original vehicle and was soon joined by a wooden-bodied ballast tractor designated FV12003 and known as Mk 1B.

The Mk 1 and Mk 2 tractors remained in service into the 'sixties, but it was pretty clear that more power was required and, in late 1958, the Mk 3 appeared. The Meteorite petrol engine was ousted in favour of a Rolls-Royce C8SFL super-charged, straight-eight diesel, producing 333bhp gross from 16,200cc. The transmission was simplified, with a six-speed main gearbox in place of the more complex 4x3 arrangement of the Mks 1 and 2. There was also a brand-new,

Above: There were times when tank transporters were pressed into other duties. This Diamond T Model 980 is hauling a barge for the crossing of the Rhine. (Tank Museum)

Left: With its huge coffin nose and stylish art deco cab, the Diamond T Model 980/981 ballast tractor managed to pull off the trick of being both stylish and useful. (Tank Museum)

and considerably more stylish, steel cab, albeit still without sleeping facilities.

The original Mk 3 was a fifth-wheel tractor, and there was also a ballast tractor, designated Mk 3A; it should be noted that it was possible to remove the ballast body and fit a fifth wheel, and vice-versa.

By the time production came to an end in 1963, total military Antar production amounted to 90 examples of the Mk 1 and Mk 2, and 105 Mk 3/3A.

SCAMMELL COMMANDER

When it came to thinking about replacing the Antars, both Scammell and Thornycroft were approached, but the Ministry of Defence was so slow in reaching a decision that by the time they had made up their minds about what was wanted, Thornycroft had been taken over by Leyland. Both firms were now, effectively, under the same ownership, with all of the Thornycroft operations located at the Scammell

During the War, a number of Diamond Ts were converted to fifth-wheel tractors to enable them to be used with similar semi-trailers to those used with the Scammell; this example also shows the open cab. (Tank Museum)

In its final, Mk 3 incarnation, the Antar acquired a diesel engine and simplified transmission; again, the vehicle was constructed as both a fifth-wheel tractor and as a ballast tractor.

plant at Tolpits Lane, Watford. However, we are getting ahead of ourselves.

In January 1968, the Fighting Vehicles Research & Development Establishment (FVRDE) had prepared a general-arrangement drawing for a 55-ton tank transporter train consisting of a three-axle tractor and twin-axle, multi-wheeled trailer; the total train weight for the anticipated vehicle, loaded, was 95 tonnes. The drawing was issued to both companies who were told that FVRDE anticipated this would be a modest upgrade rather than a wholly-new design, and the final choice of contractor was to be made by September 1969. Delivery of the first 40 of some 200 or so examples of what was being called 'Antar Mk 4' was to take place in 1971 - this was subsequently down-graded to ten vehicles delivered in 1971 for troop trials,

with production proper getting underway in October 1973.

In early 1972, the Ministry finally issued the definitive statement of requirements for a new 55-tonne tank transporter. To meet these requirements, the Scammell design team, under the direction of Don Pearson and John Fadelle, proposed a new vehicle which effectively combined the best features of the Scammell Contractor and the Thornycroft Antar.

The proposal described a semi-forward control 6x4 tractor with the engine and transmission placed over the front axle. Possible engine options included the Cummins KTA-1150, GM 12V-71, MTU MB 6V-331, and Rolls-Royce CV8-TCA; typical power outputs were in the order of 530-600bhp. Transmission was going to be either the six-speed GM-Allison 'box, or a five-speed ZF unit. All axles were

based on standard Scammell units. The five-man crew cab used Motor Panels' pressings and was to be provided with convertible sleeping/seating arrangements, using a pair of bunks.

At the end of November 1973, Scammell was appointed as prime contractor for the project. Crane-Fruehauf was selected as subcontractor for the trailer, working under the control of the Scammell team.

By late 1976, Scammell had prepared build sheets for two running engineering models - designated CT1 and CT2 - which would be submitted for trials and evaluation before the final specification was nailed down. CT1 was to be Rolls-Royce powered, CT2 would receive the Cummins unit; both would use the six-speed Allison semi-automatic transmission. The frame and rear suspension were based heavily on that used for the Contractor and, at this stage, the rear axles were to be Kirkstall Forge units as used on Scammell's 240-ton ballast tractor.

The two engineering models were completed during 1978, together with two semi-trailers, and the Rolls-Royce engined tractor was taken to the Motor Show at Earls Court in October, where it was the most expensive and most powerful vehicle on show.

Relying heavily on the client's prerogative for change, the MoD started to consider how the heavier Challenger main battle tank, which was to replace the Chieftain and Centurion, might be transported... and upped the weight classification to 65 tonnes, immediately rendering the semi-trailers obsolete. Cranes started work on designing a replacement to be ready for user trials in the autumn of 1980. By early 1980, the Scammell team believed that the preliminary tractor trials were complete and, in May, tractor CT1 was despatched to Fallingbostel, Germany for user trials. The prototype for the uprated 65-tonne semi-trailer followed in March 1981, six months behind schedule.

And then... on 25 June 1981, the Defence Secretary, John Nott, presented a series of budget cuts amounting to £200-250 million. These cuts included axing the Commander project and, on 12 January 1982, the contract was officially closed. But, by the Spring of the

The massive twin radiators of the Antar gave the vehicle an extraordinarily imposing frontal aspect.

The Mk 2 Antar was first produced as a fifth-wheel tractor for use with a semi-trailer; a wooden-bodied ballast tractor soon followed.

The Commander acquitted itself well in the Gulf War, clocking up an impressive record for reliability. (Tank Museum)

same year, it seems that the MoD Procurement Executive had miraculously found sufficient money to reinstate the project. Scammell was asked to construct the three validation vehicles which had already been planned, as well as 122 production tractors and 113 semi-trailers. The engine was to be the Rolls-Royce unit. Tractor CT1 was to be reworked to 'validation' specification but was to be abandoned once the validation trials were complete. The company had less than 16 months to complete the validation tractors and was expected to start deliveries of the first 22 production machines in April 1984.

Tractor CT1 was re-worked to the new specification and was re-designated 'TR1'. By July 1983 it was back under test with one of the 65-tonne trailers and the three new validation machines were also under test by the end of the year.

The tight schedule meant that it had been necessary to start building the production tractors before the validation trials were completed but, nevertheless, Scammell delivered the first production vehicle on 24 February 1984, with the remainder of the first batch in service by 13 June, just six weeks behind schedule. Work on the last tractor was started on 19 December 1984.

Despite the intermittent and protracted nature of the development contract, the Commanders gave fantastic service for almost 20 years.

OSHKOSH M1070F

By 1998, the MoD was starting to look for a replacement for the ageing Commanders which were nearing the end of their

Right: Although there were a small number of Commander ballast tractors, they were intended only for recovery work; for tank transporting duties the vehicle was always used with a semi-trailer.

After a long and very troubled gestation, the Scammell Commander started to enter service in 1984... here the first vehicle is being handed over to the Director General of Transport Movements.

anticipated 20-year service life. The Labour government resolved that the replacement would be purchased under the then-fashionable Private Finance Initiative (PFI) which meant that the chosen supplier would be expected to finance and supply the trucks, together with parts back-up and logistic support, and to provide crews. For its part, the government pledged to enter into a lease arrangement for a 20-year period.

This was the first such military procurement exercise to be let under the PFI, and it was intended that a decision would be made in early 2000, and that the vehicles would be supplied by 2002. Initially there were four bidders: DHT, Fasttrax, Tactacon and Hammer.

The DHT consortium (Defence Heavy Transport) consisted of the German MAN truck company and SERCo Military. Fasttrax was offering the American Oshkosh M1070

The current British tank transporter is the Oshkosh M1070F... it is effectively a 'Europeanised' version of the US Army's M1070 shown here. (Oshkosh Truck Corporation)

The British Army Oshkosh is powered by a Caterpillar C-17 engine in place of the Detroit Diesel and the power is transmitted through an Allison HD4070 automatic seven-speed gearbox, where the US tractors have a 5F1Rx2 transmission configuration. (Oshkosh Truck Corporation)

Designated M1070F, the tractor is based on the US Army's M1070 which was introduced in 1992; 1600 of these tractors are currently in service with the US Army. The British vehicles have been 'Europeanised' to meet current road traffic and 'Euro 3' emission standards, but the overall package is similar to the US machines and the vehicles were manufactured in the USA.

Major differences are in the engine and transmission. The British Army vehicles employ a Caterpillar C-17 700bhp diesel engine in place of the standard Detroit Diesel and the power is transmitted through an Allison HD4070 automatic seven-speed gearbox and Oshkosh 3000 single-speed transfer case, where the US tractors have a 5F1Rx2 transmission configuration. The driveline arrangement is 8x8 using a single driven axle at the front, with a triple bogie at the rear. The bonnet has been extended and widened to accommodate the larger engine specified by the MoD and there is a six-man crew cab.

Curiously, the truck is not dissimilar in appearance to Thornycroft's early proposals for what ultimately became the Commander. The frontal aspect is dominated by an enormous bonnet and radiator grille, whilst the cab roof is extended to form a visor over the windscreen.

The GTS 100 semi-trailer is produced by King Trailers, based in Market Harborough. It is a seven-axle design able to accommodate a payload of 72 tonnes on a bed length of 453in (17.84m), allowing either a Challenger 2 tank or two Warrior vehicles to be transported. The load is spread across 11 axles and, unladen, the vehicle width does not exceed 114in which means that the 'STGO Category 3' restrictions do not apply.

Almost 90 years after the appearance of the first tank transporter, the imminent death of the main battle tank is regularly being predicted by various military pundits. There have been five generations of British tank transporter... will the Oshkosh will be the last of its line?

tractor with a UK-built King 72-tonne semi-trailer, with finance for the deal provided by Deutsche Bank, and logistic support from Halliburton Brown & Root. Tactacon included Alvis-Unipower, Ryder Defence and PHH Vehicle Management Services, with finance by Schroders... Alvis-Unipower, incidentally, was the 'genetic' successor to Scammell. Hammer was headed by Lex Service, and proposed supplying a Foden tractor and Broshuis trailer.

Lex Service dropped out early on, leaving three bidders, and the Tactacon/Unipower bid was eliminated in late 2000, making it a straight fight between Fasttrax and DHT.

On 24 January 2001, the MoD announced that the Fasttrax/Oshkosh bid had been accepted, and that the company had 'preferred bidder' status. The contract called for 92 vehicles to be supplied by October 2003, with an option on a further 28.

Oshkosh M1070F complete with heavy armoured load... a match made in heaven!

The Glory Days of Heavy Haulage

VOLAT

Seen at IDEX 2003, the Minsk Wheeled Tractor Plant's Volat 74135 is a real monster, capable of operating at gross train weights exceeding 120 tonnes

The vehicle was something of a hit in the IDEX arena.

Produced by the Minsk Wheeled Tractor Plant (MZKT), the Volat 74135 heavy equipment tractor was one of the undoubted stars of the Abu Dhabi IDEX 2003. Although this was not its first appearance, having been displayed at the 2001 show as a static exhibit, it was the first time that the massive 8x8 truck had been seen on the move… and coupled to a 70-tonne semi-trailer and a 60-tonne drawbar trailer, both of which were fully loaded, what a sight it was! Here was a truck so large that it almost made the Oshkosh M1070 look like a toy.

MZKT's corporate heritage includes such monsters as the MAZ-535, 537 and 547 which were used as missile transporter-erector-launcher (TEL) rigs by the army of the former Soviet Union, and the plant is clearly very experienced in the design of heavy-duty all-wheel drive trucks, even to the extent of producing a 12x12 chassis for oil-field work.

The origins of the Volat 74135 tank transporter, which is intended for use in the Middle East, appear to date back to the 'nineties and, in 1999 it was reported that it was being evaluated by the United Arab Emirates. Certainly, the truck appearing at the IDEX show was carrying a UAE Leclerc main battle tank plus a couple of Soviet-built BMP-3s.

Weighing in at more than 26 tonnes, the Volat is powered by a front-mounted Deutz-MWM TBD-234 V12 turbo-charged and inter-cooled diesel engine producing a massive 788bhp from 21.6 litres; some of the company's documentation suggests that a 780bhp DaimlerChrysler OM 444-LA may also be specified as an alternative. The transmission is a joint American-Belarus project, consisting of a fully-automatic Allison M6600-AR six-speed (6F2R) hydro-mechanical gearbox coupled to a two-speed Minsk transfer box which incorporates a lockable inter-axle differential. Each of the axles also includes automatic and manual differential locks and there is an automatic central tyre-inflation system (CTIS) which operates on both the tractor and the three-axle MWTP-99941 semi-trailer.

Various features are included which are designed to allow the tractor to operate in hot, dusty environments, including high-efficiency air and oil filters, and cab air-conditioning. The special 23.5xR25XLBTL Michelin sand tyres and suspension system allow the truck to operate efficiently off the road, even in deep sand. Maximum speed is quoted as being in the order of 55mph (90km/h), with the average fuel consumption working out at slightly worse than 1.5mpg (1km/litre).

'Average fuel consumption works out at slightly worse than 1.5mpg

Here's how the Volat appeared at IDEX, towing a three-axle semi-trailer and a four-axle drawbar trailer on which were loaded two BMP-3s and a Leclerc main battle tank belonging the UAE Defence Force. (Courtesy, Victor Kulikov)

That massive bonnet covers a Deutz-MWM TBD-234 V12 turbo-charged and inter-cooled diesel engine with a displacement of 21.6 litres.

Above and below right: Official factory views showing the 74135 tractor and the standard MWTP-99941 70-tonne semi-trailer.

MZKT

Based in the Republic of Belarus, a former part of the Soviet Union, the Minsk Wheeled Tractor Plant (MZKT) was established in 1991 from the wheeled-tractor division of the Minsk Automobile Plant (MAZ). Since 1947, MAZ had been heavily involved in the production of the huge transport-erector-launcher vehicles which were used for mobile Soviet missile systems.

MZKT has successfully converted many of its former defence products into heavy-duty all-terrain tractors for commercial and civil-engineering applications, and the company currently produces a range of heavy-duty trucks with drive-lines ranging from three to 12 axles. Production of military vehicles also continues.

On 8 January 2002, Mikhail Leonov, the 48-year-old head of the Minsk Wheeled Tractor Factory, was arrested on charges of abuse of office, large-scale embezzlement, and unlawful entrepreneurial activities. If found guilty, he faces up to eight years in prison and confiscation of his property.

The spacious four-door cab incorporates a full-width bonnet and reverse-rake, divided windscreen, and has accommodation for a crew of seven. A 25-tonne German ITAG winch is mounted on the chassis behind the cab and there is also a crane for handling the spare wheels.

The 'standard' MWTP-99941 semi-trailer is rated at 70 tonnes, and has a load-bed length of 45.5ft (13.9m); the trailer is loaded via hydraulic ramps which are raised and lowered by an auxiliary power unit carried on the trailer itself. The trailer is large enough to accept a main battle tank or two armoured personnel carriers (APC) or infantry fighting vehicles. Other Russian or East European semi-trailers may also be used.

According to MZKT, the vehicle is capable of operating at gross train weights exceeding 120 tonnes... MZKT, rather charmingly, describe this monster as being a 'heavy-duty autotrain… suitable for the transportation of heavy caterpillar rigs'.

HET-70

Pat Ware takes a look at the M746, a heavy equipment transporter originally intended for use with the US-German MBT-70 main battle tank

The production versions (known as M746 and M747) manufactured by Ward LaFrance, differed from the prototype in various ways, most notably the use of a removable hard-topped cab and a turbo-charged diesel engine; note also that the air cleaners have been moved. The use of the same M60 tank load as used with the prototypes suggests that the photograph was also taken at Chrysler's Detroit Arsenal plant. (Courtesy, David Doyle)

Back in the mid-'sixties, West Germany and the USA agreed to co-operate on the design and development of a new main battle tank which could be supported by a common logistics system. Intended to enter service in the 'seventies, the project was dubbed MBT-70, and prototypes were produced armed with a version of the 152mm XM150E5 gun-launcher which was used for the US M551 Sheridan and M60A2 tanks. The prototypes were not identical, and each demonstrated differing design philosophies in various areas. At the same time, the US Chrysler Corporation, and the German companies Faun and Kruppe, were jointly developing a heavy equipment transporter (HET) for the tank which, perhaps not surprisingly, was sometimes known as the HET-70... or SLT-70 in German.

Development of the tank was slow and the plug was pulled on the MBT-70 project in 1971, with both countries choosing to go their own ways... in truth, the concept was virtually abandoned, the Germans coming up with the Leopard and the Americans with the M1 Abrams. However, the complementary transporter fared slightly better and, although no production agreement was ever concluded between the two countries, production of similar vehicles did at least take place in both the USA and Germany, albeit they were certainly not identical.

The so-called HET-70 was intended for recovering disabled tanks or other armoured vehicles, and for transporting tanks, cargo etc on communications zone supply routes... it was described as having 'limited cross-country mobility' and its main asset was its enormous power rather than out-and-out off-road performance. Most of the development work was undertaken in the USA, by the Chrysler Corporation, with the German Faun company forced to abandon work on its similar L1212/50 25-ton 8x8 tractor in favour of the American

Chrysler produced two prototypes, designated XM746, towards the end of the 'sixties.

With the low, cab-forward stance and mid-mounted engine that has subsequently become a feature of many such vehicles, this was a massive 8x8 machine, 10ft (3050mm) wide, and measuring more than 10ft (3050mm) to the cab roof. In line with normal US practice, the designers adopted a hinged

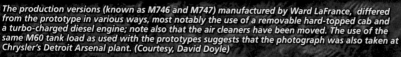

'...motor pool scuttlebutt has it that the cab could actually accommodate eight men in line abreast!'

windscreen and folding top for the four-man cab, which allowed the overall height to be reduced... and motor pool scuttlebutt has it that the cab could actually accommodate eight men in line abreast!

The tractor weighed in at 182,400 lb (20,780kg) and was nominally rated at 22 tons; with the matching 16-wheeled four-axle XM747 goose-neck semi-trailer in place, the rig measured 61ft (18.6m) from

lb (82,900kg). Although initially rated at a nominal 52 1/2 tons, it was said to be capable of accommodating armoured vehicles weighing up to 60 tons. Power was provided by a Detroit Diesel 12V-71 two-stroke diesel engine producing 492bhp from its 13,962cc, sufficient to provide a top speed of 38mph (60km/h) loaded. Drive was transmitted to the wheels via a Twin Disc electro-powershift 5F1R transmission and a single-speed transfer case with locking differential; axles were of the double-reduction type, manufactured by Rockwell, and incorporating limited-slip differentials at the rear. The two walking-beam bogies were suspended on tapered leaf semi-elliptical springs; there was power steering, and an exhaust brake was fitted to help slow the truck on downhill grades. The tyres were big 18.00-25 bar grips. Twin hydraulic winches were mounted amidships, with sufficient power for loading disabled tanks onto the semi-trailer, and a standard military fifth wheel was mounted over the forward rear axle.

By the time the truck was ready to enter production in 1971, the abandonment of the MBT-70 meant that there was little point in continuing the co-operation between the two countries. In West Germany, Faun developed the truck into production as the LH70/420-8x8 Elefant, but the similarities with the XM746 were superficial, the Elefant sharing more with Faun's original L1212/50 tractor. When the production contract was offered in the USA, Chrysler was unsuccessful, presumably pitching the price too high. The Ward LaFrance Truck Company, based in Elmira Heights, New York and best known by then for its fire appliances, was contracted to

One of Chrysler's XM746/XM747 prototypes (census number 05A01967) photographed prior to being put through its paces, probably at the Detroit Arsenal. The load is an American M60 medium tank with the M19 upgraded cupola... also constructed by the Chrysler Corporation, but never put into production. (Chrysler Corporation)

Production actually started in June 1973 and, in the end, amounted to no more than the initial 125 trucks, all of which were completed by 1976 at a reputed $146,000 each. Initially, most of the trucks were shipped to West Germany where they were intended to haul tanks across the German plains to what could well become the frontline of a war with the Soviet Union, but a number apparently served in the first Gulf War, Operation Desert Storm. A further 68 trucks were constructed for the Royal Morocco Army during 1977-78.

The production M746 differed in small details, most notably in the use of a steel reducible-height cab, which could incorporate an anti-aircraft machine-gun ring mount. The normally-aspirated Detroit Diesel engine was replaced by a turbocharged version (12V-71T), with power output up to 600bhp... and fuel consumption rated at a miserable 1.4mpg (0.51km/litre) – and this for a diesel, remember!

The M747 semi-trailer was constructed by the Consolidated Diesel Electric Corporation – better known as Condec - of Shenectady, New York.

The US Army planned that the vehicle, which was rated 'standardised A' in 1973, would have a life of 14 years. However, from 1977, the tractor started to be superseded by a militarised version of the Oshkosh J2065 tractor known as the M911. Although considerably less sophisticated than the M746, the M911 was at

least capable of operating with the same semi-trailer, which remained in service for some time longer.

Ward LaFrance finally closed its doors in 1983.

Surprisingly, there is more than one preserved example of the production tractor... chassis number 3 is at Fort Hood, Texas, and at least one (chassis number 96) is known to be resident in the UK. It has not yet been seen south of Cheshire, but we'd love to hear from the owner.

An anti-aircraft machine-gun ring mount could be fitted over the right-hand side of the cab roof. The legend 'Test Operation' on the cab front suggests that the truck has yet to be delivered. (Courtesy, David Doyle)

Note the huge air-cleaners ahead of the engine compartment... the sticky tape on the front bumper remains a mystery. (Chrysler Corporation)

Above: Photographed in the massive parade ground of the Royal Artillery Ba[...] Middle East customer, loads a Chieftain onto its Crane trailer.

SCAMMELL CONTRAC[...]
TANK TRANSPORTEI

Roy Larkin looks at one of the Scammell heavyweights that was not used by the British Army

Leaving aside the small matter of the WW2 Diamond Ts, Scammell had established itself as the sole UK supplier of heavy tank transporters… until the appearance of Thornycroft's Mighty Antar in 1949. However, just because the British Army was shopping elsewhere it didn't mean that Scammell had given up on military heavy haulage, and a militarised 6x4 Contractor tractor was sold to a number of foreign armies for the tank-transporter role. Although the standard semi-trailer was only rated at 60 tons, the military Contractor was perfectly capable of handling loads up to 250 tons providing the appropriate mechanical components were selected.

Civilian users had the choice of engines from Cummins, Rolls-Royce, Leyland and AEC, which ranged from 240 to 400bhp. The military Contractor generally used the Cummins NTK335 turbo-charged, six-cylinder unit rated at 335bhp; other engine options included the Rolls-Royce 305 and the Cummins NT370, rated at 305bhp and 370bhp, respectively. Turbo-charging was regarded as essential for operation at high altitudes, since this allowed no loss of power at elevations up to 12,000ft (3,600m) above sea level.

As regards the transmission, users could opt for the Fuller RTO-913 or RTO-915 Roadranger manual gearboxes, offering 13 or 15 speeds respectively, or the RV30 semi-automatic eight or 15-speed gearbox from Self Changing Gears. The gearing was generally selected to provide a top speed of around 35mph (59km/h) and the ability to climb a 1:5.1 gradient. Alternative ratios were obtainable by a simple workshop change, enabling a top speed of 45mph (73km/h) while being able to climb a 1:6.4 gradient. Enough fuel could be carried to provide a 300 mile (486km) range.

If a manual gearbox was selected, the engine and gearbox were coupled with a

Note the air conditioning unit on the cab roof and the winch fairlead rollers at the front.

Although structurally identical, albeit offered with more choice of engine and transmission, the civilian Contractor was rated at 240 tons, against just 60 tons for the military variant.

...olwich this Contractor, intended for a

...TOR

Equipped with an anti-aircraft gun on the cab observation hatch, this rare 6x6 Contractor was photographed at the Purbeck ranges.

Lipe Rollway 15-inch, twin-plate, air-operated clutch.

The drive axles consisted of the familiar Contractor bogie, with spiral bevel drive units and epicyclic reduction hubs. A third, lockable, differential ensured maximum traction whatever the conditions. This bogie had been well proven with the Constructor before the Contractor and on the Scammell desert and dump trucks. The front axle was the standard Contractor unit with a capacity of 18,000 lb (8,130kg); the steering was hydraulic-powered and the axle was equipped with shock absorbers and non-lubrication springs.

Scammell's long experience in the Middle Eastern oilfields provided a cooling system capable of coping with temperatures of 52°C (125°F). To achieve this, a large frontal-area radiator was used, with cast top and bottom tanks which were detachable to facilitate easy maintenance and cleaning.

While operational tanks can easily and quickly be driven onto their transporters, the role of the transporter is also to recover stricken tanks. To this end, the Contractor was equipped with a vertically-mounted drum winch mounted behind the cab. The large diameter drum helped reduce the bending stress on the 500ft (122 metres) of 1in (25mm) steel rope, increasing rope life. A 'paying-in' guide ensured even layering on the drum. A dog clutch disengaged the winch drum for 'paying-out', allowing speedy

deployment of the rope, and the winch could only be operated with the winch brake cut-out employed; this prevented run-back should the engine stall. A cut-out protected the winch or rope from overloading.

Lightweight single and double sheath pulleys with quick-release pins for emergencies were fitted with anti-friction bearings with dust seals. Use of these pulleys allowed for a 50-ton (50,800kg) line pull for recovery operations, including the facility to winch through the front of the Contractor for self-recovery.

The standard cab had seating for two, with additional crew accommodation available in a canvas-covered seating area fitted behind the cab above the winch. For hot climates, a heat shield was fitted to the roof and air conditioning was available. Further optional extras included roof-mounted searchlights, a ballast box in place of the fifth-wheel, and a choice of rope length for the winch.

The trailer coupled to the unit by way of a fully oscillating fifth-wheel. This articulated about both its fore-and-aft and lateral axes to maximise stability on uneven ground. Bump stops were fitted to the fabricated saddle assembly to prevent damage during severe articulation on uneven ground. The trailer coupled to the fifth-wheel with a 3.5in (89mm) kingpin.

The 60-ton (60,960kg) capacity trailer had a usable length of 20.5ft (6.25m) and a width of 12ft (3.65m), and was designed and built by Crane of Dereham. Although the trailer carried the famous 'CF' badge, it was possibly the last product designed entirely by Crane before the company was absorbed into the Freuhauf group. The Crane running gear had been developed over many years experience with the Iraq Petroleum Company.

Standard equipment included chain tensioners and track guides designed to

1971 Scammell sales brochure for tank transporters, including the Contractor.

SCAMMELL
TANK TRANSPORTERS AND GENERAL SERVICE
AUTOMOTIVE EQUIPMENT FOR MILITARY OPERATIONS

It was a most impressive rig, capable of pulling the heaviest loads.

adjust and suit varying types of tracks. These guides were removable to provide a flat bed on which more general cargo, such as stores or machinery, could be carried. Loading was via fold-down ramps which were adjustable for width to accommodate different sizes of tank. Hinged support legs, capable of supporting a fully-freighted trailer, were mounted on the front corners of the bed, allowing the tractor unit to be used for other trailers if necessary.

The British Army favoured the Antar as a tank transporter and used Scammell's 6x4 Crusader, rather than the Contractor, as transport for engineers' plant... leaving Scammell to look overseas for sales. These came from Australia and the Middle East.

The Contractor had already gained an enviable reputation in the Australian mining industry, and the Australian Army bought them, probably supplied in CKD form to Scammell's dealer facilities. This was Scammell's normal practice for Australia.

But the main market for the Contractor was the Middle East, where Scammell had long experience and a first-class reputation with oilfield and desert trucks. Contractors were supplied to Kuwait, Libya, Iraq and Jordan. The Jordanian Army used the Contractor to supplement and replace their

ageing Constructors, although the Crane trailer was replaced by a Dyson 30-ton multi-purpose trailer which could carry two 11-tonne M113s.

Other customers included Kenya and Israel, although the Israeli trucks wore Leyland

badges due to the political climate in the Middle East. Middle East countries would not deal with companies that supported Israel, so rather than antagonising most of their Middle East customers, Scammell badged the trucks as Leylands. █

The standard Crane trailer was a semi-beavertail affair with heavy fold-down ramps which were adjustable for width to accommodate different sizes of tank; standard equipment included chain tensioners and removable track guides.

This vehicle lacks the front towbar and fairlead rollers.

Scammell men watch as the military test the machine-gun mounting, at the same time providing a good view of the winch and fifth wheel.

The Glory Days of Heavy Haulage

'WAR IS AN UGLY THING...'

..and military vehicles don't come much uglier than the 8x8 ZIL-135L4 used by the Red Army and most of the Soviet Union's Warsaw Pact allies

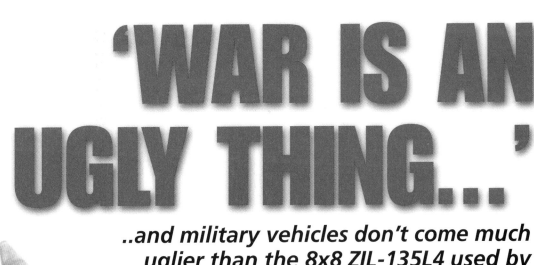

Development work on the huge 8x8 ZIL-135 chassis started in the 'sixties at the Likhachev Automobile Plant (ZIL) near Moscow. A handful of prototypes were produced at the ZIL factory – which also, incidentally, produced buses – but the vehicle was actually put into mass production in 1968 at the Bryansk Automobile Factory and, for this reason is often also referred to as the BAZ-135L4, although engines continued to be supplied by the ZIL plant. Production continued for about a decade. The truck was widely used by all of the Warsaw Pact countries – typical roles included cargo vehicle, convoy-escort gun truck, multiple launch rocket system (MLRS), and bridging vehicle. There was also a civilian pipeline carrier for oilfield projects and civil-engineering work, and an experimental 6x6 version, intended for use in snow and desert conditions, known as the ZIL-E-167. The best-known of the ZIL-135L4 variants is the missile transporter-erector-launcher (TEL). ➤

A brace of ZIL-135 transporter-erector-launchers (TEL) with their FROG-7 surface-to-surface missiles ready for launch. The FROG-7 had a range of 250 miles (430km) and could be made ready for firing in 15-30 minutes.

Rear view of a loaded ZIL-135.

This ZIL-135 appeared at War & Peace in 2001 and, for a long time, was in storage at the Kent yard of RR Services. Although the hydraulic loading crane remains in place, the missile launch rail has been removed.

The distinctive heavy 8x8 trucks started to enter service in the Soviet Union in the early-sixties, the main types being the MAZ-543, MAZ-537 and the ZIL-135L4. Primarily intended for use as missile transporter-erector-launchers, these huge trucks were the Soviet Union's first foray out of mainstream automotive design, and perhaps the first trucks produced in the USSR which were not inspired by American WW2 equipment. Although very much a product of old-school Soviet thinking as regards technology – the ZIL-135, for example, might be big and over-engineered, and is almost certainly amongst the ugliest trucks you ever saw – these are rugged and sophisticated vehicles which are designed to get the job done... regardless of prevailing conditions.

Sitting on eight massive 16.00x20 off-road tyres, and powered by a pair of seven-litre ZIL-375 V8 petrol engines, by Western standards the ZIL-135 is a monster of a vehicle, consuming fuel at a rate worse than 2mpg (160 litres/100km). The engines are the same power units as are used in the BTR-60 and the 6x6 Ural-4320 truck, producing a relatively-modest 180bhp at 3200rpm, with a total 617 lbf/ft of torque at 1800rpm. Each engine drives the four wheels on one side of the vehicle through a five-speed hydro-mechanical gearbox plus two-speed transfer case. The great fistfuls of torque available from these massive, slow-revving engines, combined with large-section tyres and a central tyre-inflation system (CTIS), which allows the driver to gain maximum traction on changing surfaces, and the maximum ground clearance under the axles of 20in (580mm), guarantees that the ZIL-135 is almost unstoppable in

Below: Watched over by 'Father Lenin', a pair of ZIL-135s parade through the Moscow streets – the date is 1977. (Viktor Kulikov collection)

Blast screens are erected over the windscreen to protect the glass when the missile is launched.

ZIL

The Soviet ZIL truck company was established in 1916 as AMO, building simple motorcars. In 1931, the factory was given a complete facelift and renamed Zavod Imjeni Stalina (ZIS); the name was changed again in 1957 when 'Stalin' was replaced by 'Likhacheva' in honour of the plant director.

The company built armoured limousines for use by the Soviet leaders, as well as trucks, buses and tanks. Motor car production ended earlier this year.

BAZ

The Bryansk Automobile Plant (BAZ) was located on the site of the former Bryansk Steel Works in Bryanskaya Oblast on the Desna River, at the western edge of what is now the Russian Federation. Production of military vehicles started in 1968 when the plant undertook production of the ZIL-135.

Current production at the plant has included the Iveco-licenced 'Gazel' van as well as a range of powerful, all-terrain trucks for military and off-road use.

The resupply vehicle carried two missiles.

the rough - in fact, the ZIL-135 was said to offer comparable off-road performance to some of the tracked Soviet vehicles.

The huge engines are housed side-by-side in a rectangular box behind the cab, with side-mounted radiators - the inset 'radiator' moulding at the cab front is presumably intended to reinforce the front panel and to provide some aesthetic effect.

Front- and rear-most axles are suspended on torsion bars, whilst the close-spaced inner axles are carried on a single fixed bogie which is attached directly to the chassis, with suspension provided only by the balloon tyres. Power-assisted steering is provided on the front and rear wheels.

The fully-enclosed snub-nosed cab is not a thing of great beauty and, although crude and unfinished to Western eyes, it is well equipped from the driver's point of view. 'Janes' claims that the cab is a three-seater but, at 110in (2,794mm), it is easily wide enough to accommodate four occupants in relative comfort. The low height to the cab roof, combined with the unusual triple windscreen, and the brutal military styling, gives the truck considerable 'presence'. ➤

(Stefan Boshniakov)

TECHNICAL SPECIFICATION

NOMENCLATURE
Truck; 10-ton, 8x8, missile launcher (ZIL-135L4, BAZ-135).

VARIANTS
Truck; 10-ton, 8x8, amphibious bridging vehicle.

Truck; 10-ton, 8x8, BM-22 multiple-rocket launcher.

Truck; 10-ton, 8x8, cargo/prime mover,

Truck; 10-ton, 8x8, convoy escort vehicle,

Truck; 10-ton, 8x8, FROG 7 missile resupply.

Truck;10-ton, 8x8, FROG 7 missile transporter-erector-launcher.

Truck; 10-ton, 8x8, SAKR-80 artillery rocket system.

Truck; 10-ton, 8x8, SSC- 1A Shaddock, or SSC-1B Sepal missile transporter/launcher.

Truck; 10-ton, 8x8, tractor.

ENGINE
Twin ZIL-375; V8; 7,000cc; overhead valves; power output (each engine),180bhp at 3,200rpm; torque (each engine), 308 lbf/ft of torque at 1,800rpm

TRANSMISSION:
5F1Rx2, hydro-mechanical; permanent 8x8.

SUSPENSION
Torsion bars on first and fourth axles; centre axles fixed.

BRAKES
Air-assisted hydraulic.

CONSTRUCTION
Steel ladder chassis with composite reinforced plastics and steel body.

ELECTRICAL SYSTEM
24V.

DIMENSIONS
Length: 365in (9,271mm)
Width: 110in (2,794mm)
Height: 99in (2,515mm)
Wheelbase: 95 + 59 + 95in (2,415 + 1,500 + 2,415mm)
Unladen weight: 19,800 lb (9,000 kg).

The use of glassfibre-resin composites for the cab and titanium-steel for the chassis keeps the unladen weight down to around nine tons, which is less than the unladen weight of an American M54 5-ton 6x6!

The rear bodywork depends on the role for which the vehicle is intended.

Cargo vehicles have a simple open box behind the engine compartment whereas those vehicles intended for use as the transporter-erector-launcher for the FROG-7 (FROG, 'free rocket over ground') missile have no bodywork to the rear, and the hydraulically-elevated rocket launcher/carrier is mounted directly to the chassis, together with a hydraulic crane mounted alongside, for lifting the missile into position. Massive hydraulic jacks, front and rear, help to stabilise the truck during launching,

and folding windscreen covers are fitted to protect the cab from backwash damage. The SSC-1A/SSC-1B Shaddock/Sepal missile TEL variants are fitted with a different cab, with the engines re-located to a forward position to provide space for the huge missile launch tube.

The FROG resupply vehicle carries three missiles, without loading/ unloading capability; crane facilities are provided on the TEL variant as well as by Ural-375 or similar trucks especially equipped for this role.

The amphibious bridging vehicle is rather in the same style as the modern western amphibious bridging systems, and carries two hinged bridge sections which can be swung out to either side of the vehicle. vehicles can be linked together to form a floating bridge system.

The Soviets have always paraded their military might on the anniversary of the 1917 Revolution. Here's a Zil-135 in parade finish, carrying a FROG-7 and taking part in a Moscow parade. (Viktor Kulikov collection)

'HERE BE DRAGONS...'

Pat Ware takes a look at the M26 Pacific Dragon Wagon – a vehicle that is certainly among the most-impressive of WW2 trucks

'**D**ragon Wagon'. With a name like that you just know that this truck is going to be something special... and, you won't be disappointed. From the huge Hall-Scott petrol engine, to the outrageous chain-drive of the Knuckey bogie, few would argue that Pacific Car & Foundry's 45-ton M26 tank transporter is the most-impressive Allied truck of WW2.

Nick-named 'Judy Mae III', this battered M26 tractor is towing a disabled Sherman. (Tank Museum)

Never happy with the British-inspired Diamond T Model 980/981, which of course was not suitable for operation in combat areas, soon after entering the War the US Army sought an alternative tractor-trailer combination for the transportation and recovery of tanks. In January 1942, the Kansas City based Dart Motor Company submitted the prototype T3 tank recovery unit to Aberdeen Proving Ground (APG) in Maryland for assessment trials. The outfit consisted of a Dart 6x6 prototype tractor – designated T13 – powered by a Waukesha six-cylinder engine. The tractor, which was a soft-skin, open-cabbed design with a long bonnet, rather in the mould of the familiar Diamond T, was coupled to the 45-ton T28 Fruehauf semi-trailer – the very same design that subsequently went into production as the M15.

Tests were being conducted on the T3 combination when, in April of that same

Restored M26 tractor coupled to an American 'Long Tom' 155mm howitzer. *(Phillip Royal)*

The stepped frame of the trailer gooseneck is very distinctive.

year, a second heavy tractor-trailer combination was submitted to APG for evaluation. This second rig consisted of a huge forward-control tractor with an armoured-cab produced by the Knuckey Truck Company of San Francisco. It was coupled to what appears to have been the same Fruehauf T28 semi-trailer – in fact, there is evidence that the development of the heavy tank transporter was actually handled through Fruehauf and that Knuckey was simply the sub-contractor chosen to produce the tractor. Never a well-known name, Knuckey specialised in custom-built heavy-duty off-road machines for use in open-cast mining and quarrying applications and, astonishingly, had apparently simply adapted the chassis of an existing vehicle, fitted the armoured cab to it, and passed it over to the Army for evaluation.

The most striking feature of the vehicle – apart from its massive size – was the angular, armoured cab which was brutal in the extreme. With the armoured shutters closed down over the radiators and the windscreen and side windows, the heavy, rhomboid shape of the cab, combined with a long 'tail', gave the vehicle the appearance of a dragon fly – which is possibly the origin of its nickname – but we should be wary of the 'Jeep' syndrome here. A platform was provided inside the cab which

allowed the use of an anti-aircraft gun on an M49 ring mount.

Power was provided by a massive Hall-Scott 400 six-cylinder petrol engine placed over the front axle, driving the patented Knuckey centre-pivoted walking-beam rear bogie through a four-speed Fuller gearbox and three-speed transfer case. The walking-beam configuration provided 18 inches (457mm) total movement from rebound to full depression of the wheels on either side. The rear axle was driven by a conventional shaft from the transfer case, with separate roller chains providing final drive to the rear wheels. The chains were kept in good fettle by means of a total-loss lubrication system, with small oil pipes dripping oil onto the chain on each side, which of course then ended up on the road!

Maximum road speed – without load – was never more than 26mph (42km/h) and little attention was paid to the comfort of the driver or six-man crew. Although, perhaps as some compensation for having to sit inside an armoured box alongside one of the world's largest petrol engines, the driver was at least given hydraulic assistance on the steering. Brakes were provided only on the rear wheels, and were operated by air pressure; separate hand controls were provided on the steering column for the brakes on either side of the tractor to help manoeuvre the massive vehicle during recovery operations.

Three winches were provided – twin 60,000 lb units at the rear, with a single 35,000 lb unit at the front; an

THE CLARKSON FACTOR

The temptation to write this piece in the style of Jeremy Clarkson was almost overwhelming but the truth is there are no superlatives or metaphors which can even begin to describe the fabled Dragon Wagon. Here is a truck that truly can snap knicker elastic from 50 paces!

At 1,090in³ – more than 17.5 litres – the six-cylinder Hall Scott engine displaces more *per cylinder* than the engine on most top-of-the-range European cars. To fill the twin 60-gallon (272 litre) fuel tanks in the UK would cost £433... and with a fuel consumption of just 1.08 miles per gallon it costs a pound every time you touch the accelerator! Power output is 240bhp at just 2,100rpm, and there is more than 800 lbf/ft of torque available – all of this transmitted to the eight rear wheels by massive roller chains.

Once the huge engine is thoroughly warmed up, the whole exhaust system glows cherry red and a three-foot flame shoots out of the vertical exhaust stack whenever the drive snaps the throttle shut for a gearchange.

Up close, it is a huge machine. The armoured cab gives the vehicle enormous brutal presence. The angular styling – if 'styling' is the right word – is like nothing else you've ever seen and could have come straight off the set of a sci-fi movie.

No matter how you approach it, this is one hell of a truck. Big, slow, thirsty, powerful, ugly... and yet so breathtaking, that the facts simply speak for themselves.

Phwoarrr...

This M26 was presumably photographed during the run-up to D-Day - the cab has been closed-down and the vehicle is carrying a DD Sherman on the original M15 semi-trailer. (Tank Museum)

The winchman's control area.

operator's platform was provided at the rear, just ahead of the spare wheel, but the front winch was operated from inside the cab. A folding 'A' frame – or 'vertical lifting device' as it was described in TM 9-767 – was carried across the chassis and the rear winches could be rigged across the frame to enable the vehicle to act as a recovery unit. Ancillary equipment included oxygen and acetylene bottles for cutting and welding, rigid drawbars for towing, a whiffletree for use with the recovery equipment, and the usual complement of pioneer tools and maintenance/repair equipment. A single spare wheel – suitable for either the tractor or trailer - was carried behind the cab on the right-hand side, with a small crane provided for handling.

A large-diameter, semi-automatic 'universal' fifth wheel coupling was placed slightly aft of the centreline of the rear bogie and was intended to couple to Fruehauf's 45-ton eight-wheel semi-trailer. This semi-trailer was a similarly-massive affair, stepped up at the front to the fifth wheel, with the near-flat trackways loaded via folding ramps at the rear. Unusually, the twin wheels on either side could be moved closer together or further apart to accommodate different widths of AFV. Despite the nominal 40 (short) ton rating of the trailer, it was frequently overloaded and, even before upgrading to 'A1' and 'A2' configuration (see below), was apparently perfectly capable of carrying loads up to 50 tons.

The two machines were tested at APG, with the Knuckey emerging as the winner – one of the deciding factors apparently being the forward-control layout and the walking-beam, chain-drive bogies. Although there were the inevitable detail changes, essentially the tractor that was put into production was very close to the prototype. Unfortunately, Knuckey lacked the production facilities required to turn-out the quantities demanded by the US Army and the production contract was awarded to the Pacific Car & Foundry Company

Left: With the 'A' frame erected over the rear bogie, the tractor could be used as a heavy recovery vehicle. The men seem to be completely oblivious to the shell bursts around them which would suggest that this is a posed shot. (Tank Museum)

Right: The cab includes a ring mount for an anti-aircraft machine gun. (Phillip Royal)

Hall-Scott

The Hall-Scott Motor Car Company could trace its origins back to 1910 when E J Hall and Bert Scott started to produce petrol-powered railcars – which, rather confusingly for us, they dubbed 'motor cars'.

However, prior to embarking on this venture with Scott, Hall had designed and constructed a number of petrol engines and when the railcar business proved slow, Hall-Scott started building engines for the aircraft industry. During the Great War the Company was involved with Jesse Vincent of Packard on the design of the so-called 'Liberty Motor' - a family of engines, of four, six, eight and 12 cylinders with common cylinder dimensions and interchangeable parts.

Bearing in mind their later involvement with Pacific Car & Foundry when Hall-Scott supplied engines for the M26 tractor, it is ironic that the Company was acquired by the rival American Car & Foundry in 1925.

In the years leading up to WW2, Hall-Scott produced engines for both marine and road vehicles including the overhead cam Invader and the 12-cylinder Defender, which was derived from it. In 1940, Hall-Scott introduced what it hoped would be a successful truck engine both for OEM applications and for operators looking for a little extra power. Dubbed the Model 400, and described as 'the most-powerful truck engine built', the unit had a displacement of 1090in³ (17,861cc) and produced a very-impressive 286bhp.

It was this engine which formed the basis for the military Model

The Hall-Scott 440 petrol engine must have been one of the largest ever to be fitted into a road-going vehicle.

440, the power unit for the M26 and, during the War, production reached a total of 2116 units, all of which were supplied to Pacific Car & Foundry.

The Company was not in good shape at the end of WW2 and the rising popularity of diesel engines ate into their market share. Following what we would now call a management buyout in 1954, the engine division was purchased by Hercules Motors Corporation in 1958 and by 1960, although some of the Company's designs remained in production, the name had disappeared.

based in Renton, Seattle – a company better known for producing railway locomotives – the 'car' in the name referring to railcars.

The tractor which Pacific Car & Foundry produced was described by the Company as the TR-1. It retained all of the salient features of the prototype, although the seven-man armoured cab did lose some of its original uncluttered appearance, the general shape and layout was unchanged. The original Hall-Scott Model 400 engine was replaced by the purpose-built military Model 440 and Knuckey's involvement continued through the supply of the massive rear bogies.

The design was standardised in June 1943 but, in mid-1944, the semi-trailer was modified to accept loads up to 45 (short) tons – designated M15A1 – and then as the 50-ton M15A2. Design changes included widening the trailer bed and providing hinged 'bridge' ramps to allow wider AFVs to pass over – rather than between – the rear wheels.

The massive rear bogie showing the chain drive to the rear wheels.

By 1944, the tactical advantages of the armoured cab no longer outweighed the weight penalty and, in October 1944, an open-cabbed unarmoured version of the tractor was standardised as the M26A1 and the original, armoured variant, was downgraded to 'limited standard'. It would be an exaggeration to say the M26A1 lacked the brutal good looks of its armoured sibling but, at the same time, it lost a certain amount of 'presence'.

The British Fighting Vehicle Proving Establishment used a modified Dragon Wagon tractor during the development of the still-born FV1000 and FV1200 projects. Nicknamed 'Big John', it was fitted with single rear wheels and over-sized tyres. (IWM, MVE17110/5)

Total production between 1943 and 1945 amounted to 1,372 vehicles and many remained in Europe after the War, the French particularly taking to it with great enthusiasm. Surplus Dragon Wagons were also a popular conversion for heavy-haulage operators.

Bearing in mind the size of the beast, a surprising number are in the hands of enthusiasts.

The soft-skin M26A1 variant lacked the brutal good looks of its armoured sibling – the loose spare wheel makes this look like an 8x8. (Maarten Swarts)

Truck stop

The British Army's current tank transporter is the American-built Oshkosh M1070F, an 18-litre Cummins-engined monster capable of easily handling loads approaching 100 tons. The wire cage surrounding the cab is designed to deter would-be grenade throwers... a necessary precaution in Iraq and Afghanistan.

18·KM·19

Since the early 'thirties, the British Army has used just four heavy tank transporters. The Scammell Pioneer, the US-built Diamond T Model 980/981, the Thornycroft Antar, and the Scammell Commander. With the Commander about to be replaced by a fifth generation of tank transporter, in the shape of the American Oshkosh M1070F heavy equipment transporter, we thought that perhaps it was time to take a look at the story of the Commander in a little more depth.

By 1968, the Antar had been in service for some 20 years, albeit through three 'marks'. The diesel-powered Mk 3/3A, introduced in 1961, had given the vehicle a useful increase in life expectancy, but it was, nevertheless, clearly starting to show its age. With a tank on board, it was slow by modern standards – which must have made it something

Leyland empire and both companies were asked to pitch for the work.

In January 1968 the Fighting Vehicles Research & Development Establishment (FVRDE) had prepared a general-arrangement drawing for a 55-ton tank transporter train consisting of

This is how it started. Scammell's scale model of a short-bonnetted 6x4 tractor with twin-axle multi-wheel 55-tonne trailer.

a three-axle tractor and twin-axle, multi-wheeled trailer. The drawing was issued to both companies who were told that FVRDE anticipated that this would be a modest upgrade rather than a wholly-new design. The total train weight for the anticipated vehicle, loaded, was 95 tonnes, distributed as 13.4 tonnes on the front axle, 35.4 tonnes on the tractor bogie and 46.2 tonnes on the trailer wheels. The 'Antar Mk 4', as they were describing

of an embarrassment on the German autobahns – and there was increased sensitivity regarding its excessive axle loadings. When overloaded or pulling very hard, it also had a nasty habit of depositing the entire contents of the rear axle casing, gears and all, on the road which did not endear it to the German civil authorities.

However, when the Ministry of Defence (MoD) started to cast around for a more modern replacement in early 1968, it seemed logical that they should go knocking on Thornycroft's door again. In fact, it would probably be fairer to say that they went knocking on the door of Leyland Specialised Vehicles because both Thornycroft and Scammell now formed part of the

it, was scheduled to enter service sometime in 1971.

The companies were allocated less than five months to complete their specifications, with the all of the various discussions – both technical and commercial – due to be concluded by September 1968. The final choice of contractor was to be made by September 1969 with delivery of the first 40 of some 200 or so vehicles taking place in 1971 – this was subsequently down-graded to ten vehicles delivered in 1971 for troop trials, with production proper getting underway in October 1973.

The final treatment for the bonnet was proposed by John Beck, a freelance industrial designer working for Leyland. Although the grille treatment is not yet finalised – and the bonnet was later given a raised lip at the rear to aid cooling – this is more-or-less how the finished tractor was to look.

COMMANDER

An in-depth look at the tortuous development saga of the Scammell Commander

Everyone believed that the timescale was tight and that there was no room for any slippage although, as it happened, it was hardly mattered for it was not until May 1973 that FVRDE finally got around to producing the detailed 'statement of requirements'. During the intervening five year, Thornycroft had done all that they could in choosing engine, transmission, axle and tyre suppliers and then had presumably lost hope and filed the project away somewhere.

There are several reasons for the delay, not least of which was the fact that in April 1970 FVRDE was merged with Military Engineering Experimental Establishment (MEXE) to form the Military Vehicles and Engineering Establishment (MVEE). At much the same time that the boffins were busy screwing new nameplates to their office doors, Thornycroft was fully absorbed into the Leyland leviathan and all of its operations were moved to the Scammell plant at Tolpits Lane, Watford.

Scammell had also presumably been working on outline designs for the new tank transporter but when the Thornycroft design team pitched up at Watford, what they managed to produce between them was effectively the offspring of the Scammell Contractor and the Thornycroft Antar.

Once the Antar Mk 4 name was dropped, there was actually a period when the project was called the Contractor Mk 3.

In early 1972, MVEE issued SR55, the definitive statement of requirements for a new 55-tonne tank transporter – note that it was now firmly metricated.

It was clear that Thornycroft's earlier work was no longer adequate and, under the direction of Don Pearson and John Fadelle, the design team literally went back to the drawing board spending the best part of a year in drawing-up a

Once Scammell had been selected as the prime contractor, this full-size wood and glass-fibre mock-up was produced – note the name 'Contractor' on the bonnet.

feasibility study. Whilst the document described and illustrated 14 different tractor configurations, each of which was compared to the MVEE requirement, it came down in favour of a semi-forward control 6x4 tractor with the engine and transmission placed over the front axle. Possible engine options included the Cummins KTA-1150, GM 12V-71, MTU MB 6V-331, and Rolls-Royce CV8-TCA; typical power outputs were in the order of 530-600bhp. Transmission was going to be either the six-speed GM-Allison CLBT-6061 or a five-speed ZF unit. All axles were based on standard Scammell units, although there

was some doubt regarding the ability of the front axle to withstand the specified braking performance.

The five-man crew cab was based on Motor Panels pressings and was to be provided with convertible sleeping/seating arrangements using a pair of bunks. A small scale model was produced to demonstrate the possible appearance of the machine.

The feasibility study was issued in May 1973, but it took almost six more months before the MoD appointed Scammell as prime contractor for the project. Crane-Fruehauf was selected as subcontractor for the trailer, working under the control of the Scammell team.

In late 1976 Scammell produced a full-size mock-up of the tractor in wood and glass-fibre – by this time, although the short bonnet had been lengthened, the overall appearance was not

CT2 was all-but destroyed by fire during 1980 - this is all that remained and the decision was taken not to rebuild it. (Tank Museum)

dissimilar to the earlier model. The mock-up was very effective at demonstrating the (somewhat ungainly) appearance of the beast in a way that was not possible with a small-scale model, but most importantly, it showed how the major automotive components would be accommodated.

At about the same time, Scammell prepared build sheets for two running engineering models effectively derived from the Contractor – designated CT1 and CT2 – which would be submitted for trials and evaluation before the final specification was nailed down. CT1 was to be powered by a Rolls-Royce engine, CT2 would receive the Cummins unit but, the Scammell team favoured the American-made Cummins. Both would use the six-speed Allison semi-automatic transmission. The frame and rear suspension were based heavily on that used for the Contractor and, at this stage, the rear axles were to be Kirkstall Forge units as used on Scammell's 240-ton ballast tractor.

The Scammell team was still concerned about MVEE's demand for 60% (Tapley) braking efficiency and requested a separate sum of money to conduct braking trials. During 1976, a test rig was assembled using a Cummins-engined Contractor chassis and this spent ten or 12 weeks with 414 Squadron Royal Corps of Transport undergoing road trials.

As regards the cab, the decision was taken to stick with the Motor Panels unit but John Beck, a freelance industrial designer, was asked to take a look at the front end, and particularly, the treatment of the radiators. He came up with an attractive model which lengthened the bonnet still further and effectively defined the

appearance of what became the Commander.

During 1978 the two engineering models were completed, together with two semi-trailers. The tractors were

The final choice of power unit was between the Cummins KTA-1150 and the Rolls-Royce CV8-TCA. The photograph shows the Rolls-Royce engine.

registered 06SP02 and 06SP04 whilst the trailers were given the numbers 06SP03 and 06SP05. The Rolls-Royce engined tractor was taken to the (combined motor car and commercial vehicle) Motor Show at Earls Court in October, where it was the most expensive and most powerful vehicle on show. Once the motor show was out of the way, it was intended that the two engineering models would clock-up 60,000 miles between them on the various test tracks and circuits used by

MVEE. The target for 'mean distance between battlefield failures' was 3,000 miles.

It was also at about this time that the MoD started to consider how the heavier Challenger main battle tank, which was to replace the Chieftain and Centurion, might be transported. The weight classification was upped to 65 tonnes, and although the tractor was fine, the increase immediately rendered the semi-trailers obsolete. Cranes started work on designing a replacement which was scheduled to be ready for user trials in the Autumn of 1980.

By early 1980, the Scammell team believed that the user trials were complete and called a meeting to discuss some 423 incident reports which had been compiled during the running of both the tractors and trailers. Aside from structural failures in the yet-to-be-upgraded trailers, there were no serious problems remaining unresolved. The Rolls-Royce

Although this is not referred to in the text, the Commander was also almost supplied to Iran before the fall of the Shah in 1979. This vehicle is a third engineering model which was produced for trials in Iran – it differs in detail to the British Army tractors.

engine was removed from CT1 and sent back to the makers to be stripped and assessed for wear. There was no similar examination for the Cummins engine of tractor CT2 since it, and most of the tractor, had been destroyed by an electrical fire during the trials.

In May 1980, tractor CT1 was despatched to Number 7 Tank Transporter Regiment at Fallingbostel, Germany for user trials. This was not only a means of assessing the technical reliability of the equipment under service conditions, but was also a way of ensuring that it did not present any practical problems in use. Many detailed points arose during the four-month test period but none was sufficiently serious to bring the programme to a halt or to have any serious effect on the anticipated completion date.

The prototype for the uprated 65-tonne semi-trailer was available in March 1981 and, six months behind schedule, was submitted for trials. At the same time, Scammell was pressing the MoD for a decision on which engine was to be used since this would allow them to complete the re-working of tractor CT1 and to construct three more examples for what was called the 'validation build'.

No decision had been made when, on 25 June 1981, John Nott presented a series of defence cuts to Parliament amounting to £200-250 million. Unfortunately, the Commander project was axed as part of this review – never mind that the Antars were not getting any younger and that the tanks were clearly not getting any lighter.

On 12 January 1982, the contract was officially closed.

No-one involved in the project

Showing off its handsome, purposeful lines, this may well be the first Commander to actually have been completed. Photographed in September 1983.

The British Army had no recovery vehicle capable of dealing with a disabled Commander. To get around the problem, 12 steel ballast bodies were constructed under a separate contract; these removable bodies could be fitted over the fifth wheel of any tractor to produce a powerful towing vehicle. A ballast-bodied tractor usually accompanies any operational convoy of Commanders.

TECHNICAL SPECIFICATION

NOMENCLATURE
Tractor, wheeled, semi-trailer, 98 tonne GCW, 6x4, LHD; Scammell S25 Commander.
  Some tractors were retro-fitted with steel ballast bodies for recovery but they were not identified separately and the body remained removable.

ENGINE
Rolls-Royce CV12-TCE; 12 cylinders in 60° 'V' formation; 26,110cc; overhead valves; twin turbo-chargers; power output, 625bhp at 2,100rpm; torque, 1,680 lbf/ft at 1,400rpm.

TRANSMISSION
GM-Allison CLBT-6061, semi-automatic; 6F1R; 6x4.

SUSPENSION:
Live axles on semi-elliptical multi-leaf springs.

BRAKES
Air pressure; pedal-operated hydraulic retarder fitted to gearbox.

CONSTRUCTION
Channel-section steel ladder chassis with pressed-steel body and glass-fibre composite bonnet.

ELECTRICAL SYSTEM
24V.

DIMENSIONS
Length: tractor 355in, complete train 750in
Width: tractor 124in, semi-trailer 145in
Height: 132in.
Wheelbase: 198in
Bogie centres: 63in.
Weight: tractor47,960 lb; complete train 81,840 lb.

allowed themselves to believe that this was really the end, and there was a period of hiatus during which was Scammell demonstrated 'off-the-shelf' S24 and S26 commercial tractors to the MoD in an attempt to convince them that there was no real alternative to completion of the Commander project.

By the Spring of 1982 it seems that the MoD Procurement Executive had miraculously found sufficient money somewhere – perhaps they cut

The Glory Days of Heavy Haulage

Surprisingly, at least one Antar Mk 2 remained in service after the Commanders were delivered in 1984 - it is seen here loaded onto the Commander's semi-trailer presumably for disposal.

Major-General W L Whalley hands over the keys of the first production Commander to Major-General D H Braggins on 24 February 1984.

Here's one that didn't quite make it back from the Gulf War in one piece. Unipower - who purchased the rights to continue to produce certain Scammell products - undertook to rebuild the most severely-damaged examples.

expenditure elsewhere – to reinstate the project.

A letter of intent was issued which asked Scammell to construct the three validation vehicles which had already been planned, as well as 122 'production' tractors and 113 semi-trailers. The engine was to be the Rolls-Royce unit. Tractor CT1 was to be reworked to 'validation' specification but was to be abandoned once the validation trials were complete. Of course, everything was wanted in a desperate hurry now. Scammell had less than 16 months to complete the validation tractors and was expected to start deliveries of the first 22 production machines in April 1984.

Tractor CT1 was re-worked to the new specification and was re-designated 'TR1'. By July 1983 it was back at MVEE under test with one of the 65-tonne trailers. The three new validation machines were under test by the end of the year.

Minor problems continued to emerge during these trials and there were some heart-stopping moments when all four tractors suffered failure of the leading drive axle. Eventually this turned out to be due to the bearing races being distorted as a result of being pressed into a slightly oval housing but the problem was not actually solved until after the first production machines had been delivered.

The tight schedule meant that it had been necessary to start building the production tractors before the validation trials were completed but, as good as their word, Scammell delivered the first production vehicle – registered 52KB57 – on 24 February 1984, with the remainder of the first batch in service by 13 June, just six weeks behind schedule. Work on the last tractor was started on19 December 1984.

Development work had cost somewhere in the region of a million pounds and each production tractor – with its trailer – cost £218,000 in 1984. Although this is a considerable sum of money, the Commander was clearly money well spent - with just a single mid-life rebuild, the tractors have seen 20 years continuous service and have been 'deployed to war' in the Middle East twice.

Scammell and their successors Unipower are now long gone, as is most of the domestic heavy truck industry, and it will be a sad day when the last Commander is driven away, either to its new home - possibly, and ironically, in the Middle East - or to the scrappie.

Here, the convoy passes through typical northern town – complete with cobbled surface and tramlines. Note the rare Hillman utility by the side of the road.

In the early 'fifties the Australian Government finally decided on one of the largest irrigation projects ever attempted in the world. It must be remembered that Australia is the world's driest country, and what was to be known as the Snowy Mountain Scheme in New South Wales involved the complete reversal of the Snowy River from flowing eastwards into the Pacific to westwards into the interior, and to join it with two existing rivers, the Murrumbidgee and the Murray. The scheme entailed the construction of 16 dams, almost 100 miles of tunnel blasted through solid rock and the building of seven underground power stations. 100,000 workers from around the world worked for nearly 25 years to complete the project.

The contractor realised early on that a complete tractor-trailer

outfit of some 120-ton capacity would be required, and accordingly approached the Road Haulage Association (RHA) in London, seeking advice from an established heavy haulage concern as to which was the best combination to purchase. The RHA put the Australians in contact with Wynns.

In March 1951, we had just put the first 16-wheel hydraulic suspension trailer into service. Built by Cranes of Dereham, we knew it would be ideal, and we were pleased to recommend it to the Australians. They placed an order with Cranes for what was the third trailer of this type. We had also just put the first of our six rebuilt Pacific M26 tractors on the road, but thought it best to advise them to choose Scammell Constructors. However – and I must assume that price became a consideration – they opted for the Thornycroft Mighty Antar.

The Mighty Antar had been developed in 1949 for hauling sections of steel oil pipe across the Iraqi desert from Homs to Kirkuk, but had quickly been snapped up by the British Army as an 'off the shelf' tank transporter. The first British Army Antars were steel-bodied ballast tractors but in 1952 Thornycroft started work on developing the Mk 2 military Antar which was eventually produced in both fifth-wheel and ballast tractor form. Perhaps it was the use of the Antar as a tank transporter that impressed the Australians but, whatever the reason, a contract was placed for a pair of wooden-bodied ballast tractors – chassis numbers 54780 and 54781 – similar to the military Mk 2 specification. Like the military versions, these two tractors were powered by the huge Rover V8 Meteorite engine – in compression-ignition configuration rather than the fuel-injected petrol version favoured by the British Army. Transmission was the standard Thornycroft 4F1Rx3 arrangement which put 12 speeds at the disposal of a nimble driver who had learned the art of split changing. A 50,000 lb Darlington winch was fitted behind the cab; air-brake connections were provided at front and rear for double-heading and, unusually, the connections were conveniently placed to allow the brakes to be operated whilst the tractors were pushing the massive trailer sideways.

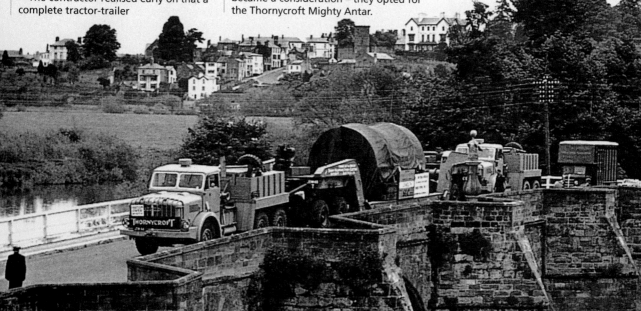

SNOWY MOUNTAIN A

John Wynn describes his company's involvement in trialing the two T
tractors destined for moving equipment on the massive Australian S

The two Antar tractors were used to push-and-pull the massive stator on the Cranes trailer. Often there wasn't much we could do about the resulting traffic queue...

...but whenever we had the opportunity we would pull over and allow the build-up of traffic to pass.

Manoeuvering the vehicles through narrow streets was always something of a challenge - and one which our Australian colleagues felt was better left to us.

It was arranged that the Australian crew would come over to the UK since the contractor, quite naturally, wanted to have the outfit road-tested before being exported. We had secured an order for six 120-ton inner stators from GEC at Whitton, Birmingham to the Uskmouth A power station in our home town of Newport. This was on schedule for transport. So we drove the Australian crew up to Birmingham over the road that they would have to travel. We had taken delivery of the Antar tractors and 120-ton Cranes trailers on their behalf and parked them in the works. To operate legally in the UK, both tractors had to be licensed and the two plates were JDW 48 and JDW 49.

On seeing the route – no motorways in those days, of course – they prudently asked if one of our crews would bring the outfit down and they would ride with us. As I recall, Bill Pitton drove the lead tractor and Wilf Wedlake the pusher – Kipper Kent was the steersman. The journey was accomplished without incident, but negotiating a notorious corner at Monmouth was, as always, a very tricky manoeuvre, with the front tractor uncoupled to gain maximum headroom, as the photograph below shows.

I must say that neither of our drivers was greatly impressed with the Antars but, in all fairness, they were the first in production and, of course, our Cummins-powered Pacifics, with their forward-control configuration, were without equal at the time.

Readers interested in learning more about the Australian Snowy Mountain Scheme, can view it on the Sky Discovery Channel – listed as 'Super Structures'. There is a fleeting shot of the two solo tractors still with their British number plates.

A lovely juxtaposition - 'Ye Olde English Tea Shoppe' and 120-ton Cranes trailer with its massive load.

NTARS

croft Antar
Mountains Scheme

PACIFICATION!

Nick Larkin describes the restoration of a very rare Pacific M26 tractor – not into military guise, but into that of its post-war role with Wynn's Heavy Haulage.

Photographs by Nick Larkin

No wonder there was so much anticipation in the air – as if we were awaiting a royal visitor or even a *Coronation Street* celebrity. Everyone was looking forward to seeing for real a star most had only previously admired in black-and-white photographs. Finally the time had arrived.... we heard her before they opened the roller shutter doors – and she sounded like thunder. Finally, the door rose to reveal ... the ex-Wynn's Pacific, 'Enterprise', in all its huge gleaming red glory.

She roared onto the rally field, the clicking of cameras drowned by the supercharged Cummins engine, and when she was finally parked, the huge Pacific was besieged by admirers. It was an event of raw emotion for many, not least former operator John Wynn, who hadn't sat in the cab for 30 years. "I well remember driving this vehicle and feel so at home in here, though I can't believe this Pacific has finally been restored. It looks wonderful," he said.

The day was also a milestone for present owner Mike Lawrence, who'd bought the beast in a sorry state 21 years earlier. The unveiling appropriately took place at Mike's Vintage Hay and Harvest rally on his Somerset farm, an event raising money for the National Blind Children Society.

Many people had helped with the complex restoration of the Pacific, which dwarfed tractors, lorries, people – in fact, everything – at the event. But, just like the restoration, it's difficult to know where to start with the story of this incredible vehicle. Elsewhere in this book we have covered the development of the Pacific M26, or 'Dragon Wagon', but after the War, many Pacifics were used in heavy haulage, and a few of these vehicles

spent more years in 'civvy' service than were ever spent hauling tanks.

None were more famous than the fleet bought by Wynn's.

Soon after the end of the War, John Wynn's father, H P Wynn, had heard of two dozen surplus Pacifics stored for sale in a Kent quarry. He went to take a look at them and ended up buying six for use, and a further four for spares.

Recalls John Wynn, "I can remember we paid about £400 each for them – a fraction of the cost of a new Scammell. After stripping off the armoured cabs – there was about eight tons of armoured steel which we sold at a good profit, obviously – we put the vehicles through the workshops and built new soft-skin cabs. Although they looked the same, there were never any measurements – they were all done on the floor and our carpenters did a wonderful job."

The rebuilds took place over a 14-year period as the vehicles were needed, the first appearing in September 1950 and the last, the star of this feature, making its debut in December 1964.

John thought up names for all the vehicles – Dreadnought, Helpmate, Conqueror, Challenger and Enterprise. The only difference between the vehicles is that two (including Enterprise) had a back bogie 114in wide, against 123in wide on the other four.

Head-on, the Pacific looks as if nothing could stand in its way.

As manufactured, the Pacifics were fitted with a six-cylinder 17.85 litre Hall-Scott petrol engine. John Wynn recalls that "they were good engines, and had wonderful pulling power, but they'd only do about three gallons to the mile! We tried the Hercules diesel from the Diamond T in some of the early conversions but 'Enterprise' was fitted with a Roots super-charged Cummins 320 engine, which we bought reconditioned from Blackwood Hodge, Northampton, who were Terex and Euclid main dealers." The unit in Enterprise is believed to have originally been in a 'fifties Euclid. The Pacific's original four-speed gearbox was also replaced – in this case, with an eight-speed unit built by Self-Changing Gears.

Enterprise was withdrawn in 1973, and eventually landed up Sullivan's yard at Bedhampton, where Mike Lawrence became rather a fan of the machine. "I've always liked big vehicles and I used to visit from time to time. I remember that the Pacific just stood there in the yard and I recall looking up at it thinking, "That's a great ugly thing..." Mike also remembers

asking Mr Sullivan what he wanted for it and that the amount was too much money for what would essentially be a bit of a plaything. "He also had a very early low-loader trailer that had belonged to Norman Box and both were on offer when

an auction was held. I went with an open mind, and ended up with the Pacific."

That was in 1982, and it would be a further 17 years before efforts were made to start the engine. Mike recalls, "When I bought it I didn't think a lot about it at the

Thankfully, the diffs were in good condition and the massive axles – this is the front – only needed draining and refilling.

'Will it fit in your garage?' – almost certainly not!

The selector unit for the eight-speed Self Changing Gears transmission which was used to replace the original Fuller crash box.

time. John Wynn wrote a piece in *Truck and Driver* magazine in 1988 and said there was a Pacific (this one!) crying out for restoration. I remember thinking I must do something about it.

"The Pacific stood in our yard and, to be honest, the condition hadn't been good when we got it, but it got worse, though various jobs such as a gearbox rebuild were carried out and other things were done when there were people who could turn their hand to them. My son Ross starting doing bits when he was 10 or 11.

"Once the engine was started we discovered that there was a nasty crack in the block, although, luckily, it could be repaired with chemical metal.

"Other tasks were completed over the years, but it wasn't until October 2002 that the final thrust began. Several of us were having a cup of tea one Sunday afternoon and got on to the subject of the Pacific. People wanted to start there and then but I thought it was too late at 4pm. Next

thing, the Pacific had been pushed into the workshop with a tractor and we never looked back.

"First job was to tackle the ballast boxes which Wynn's had fitted in place of the original fifth wheel. Most of the framework was OK although there were some areas that needed repair – and then we fitted new steel panels as needed.

"Lifting off the ballast-box framework to get at the chassis revealed a nasty surprise. As you all know by now, the Pacific has a chain drive to the rear wheels and these are lubricated by drip-feed oilers. Over the years the oil had dried so hard we had to use an air chisel to get some of it off. Nothing else would touch it. We took the hubs and wheels off on one side. Just to clean the rear axle, the hubs and the chassis from the gearbox took 14-15 hours of steam cleaning – and that was a steam cleaner with a very short nozzle on it! Thankfully the chains themselves were generally in good condition, apart

from one needing some new sections making up.

"The suspension needed very little attention – there are no springs at the rear, just shock absorbers, but the front leaf springs had survived well.

"Next it was time to get to work on the cab, with attention being needed to framing at the rear." Then came a none-too pleasant discovery, as Mike recalls, "The timbers in the roof looked perfectly good, but the aluminium cladding had been put on with small panel pins. The wet had sort of followed these in and rotted the wood."

All this had to be replaced, with Ron Skinner carrying out the work. The back of the cab was re-skinned in aluminium and the roof resealed. Other panels were replaced as necessary.

"New mudguards had to be made using what was left of the originals as a pattern. Two in One Ducting of Cheddar did an excellent job here."

The inside of the cab was etch primed, given two coats of undercoat and repainted. Mike explained that the cab had been equipped with whatever instruments Wynn's could buy in 1963 and some of these needed replacement. Indicators and lights were picked up at the Classic and Vintage Commercial Show at Donnington, and windscreen motors and arms from the Donnington Steam Fair.

Now to the painting. The chassis was painted with red oxide and then sprayed with Tractol paint in Massey Ferguson Silver Mist. "Because the Pacific is so big, we were just using tin after tin after tin of paint," Mike recalls. The cab was rubbed down to bare metal, etch primed, then primed with five coats of Hi-Build red oxide, followed by five coats of Post Office Red top coat. Sign-writing was entrusted to Graham Booth, who owns two Wynn's Scammells, and he did a great job.

The list of mechanical jobs included doing something about the compressor, which was cracked with frost damage. This was eventually replaced with one from a Cummins-powered Volvo F88. The clutch on the engine appeared to be the original – an American Lipe unit – and this was

There's not a lot of space for the driver considering vehicle's size. Steering wheel is the original and the instruments are basically those available to Wynn's in 1963.

Pacific's owner Mike Lawrence, left, with John Wynn.

Like all its sister vehicles, Wynn's gave this Pacific a name - others were called Dreadnought, Helpmate, Conqueror and Challenger.

repaired. The brakes were stripped and overhauled with Westinghouse cylinders and new rollers... but there was no point in trying to do anything about the front brakes because there aren't any. The axles were drained and fluid replaced, and the starter motor was replaced. The supercharger was in good working order.

New tyres were fitted on the front, costing £220 each from Kings Road Tyres of Ilminster – Mike had been quoted £300 from one firm way back in the 1980s. Nothing went wrong with the tyres or the fitting, but then disaster struck!

"We took the wheels down to the fitters shotblasted and brought them back painted. I loaded them into the back of my pick-up, which I left outside my workshop overnight. The pick-up was stolen and the wheels had gone as well. The pick-up was later found abandoned in a field – but the wheels weren't there. We spent a lot of time and had an appeal on local radio. A week later a man who works for a plant hire firm stopped in a lay-by and saw what he thought were pipe rims... happily, he had found the Pacific's wheels."

Finally, and with Mike's event looming, the Pacific was ready to

show, Mike's event being very much a Wynn's reunion.

"We'd been building up to this for a long time and when we actually drove it out I must admit I was quite emotional. All those years I'd kept on thinking we must do it and finally we had.

"There's actually still some work to do to the electrics and ballast-box floor so we won't be rallying the

Pacific this year. Next year we hope to take it to events. After all this, we want to have some fun with the vehicle – we want a lot of people to enjoy seeing it. That would definitely give us pleasure."

Early colour photographs of 'Enterprise' taken whilst in service with Wynn's. (Photos courtesy of Mike Lawrence)

Counting Chickens...

In the late 'nineties, Unipower was confident that the MH8875 would be selected as the British Army's future tank transporter but, as so often happens, even the best laid plans are apt to go awry

THE British Army's first heavy tank transporter was the Scammell Pioneer dating from 1939. At just 30-tons rating, it was scarcely adequate even at the time and in 1942 was virtually superseded by the Diamond T Model 980/981. In turn, it was planned that the Diamond T would be replaced by the 30-ton FV1200 and 60-ton FV1000 tractors but when these projects fell by the wayside, a version of the civilian Thornycroft Mighty Antar was pressed into service. The Antar was modified through three 'marks', to become a very competent vehicle but the weight of AFVs, and particularly main battle tanks, continued to rise inexorably during its years of service, and by the early-seventies was clearly showing its age. The War Office approached Thornycroft to discuss developing an Antar Mk 4 and, although some early design studies were produced, when Thornycroft was swallowed up by the Leyland empire, the project ended up with Scammell, albeit under some of the Thornycroft team. So by 1972, it seemed that the wheel had turned a full circle.

The Rolls-Royce CV12-TCE powered Commander was derived from a vehicle first designed for Iraq and was effectively the son of the Antar Mk 3 and the Scammell Contractor and, although it upped the ante considerably in terms of performance and pulling power, was very much in the same mould as its parents. The gestation period was long and painful and the project was cancelled by the Ministry of Defence (MoD) more than once but at last, in 1984, the British Army took delivery of the first of 125 Scammell Commanders - the fourth generation of heavy tank transporters.

Given a mid-life rebuild in the early-nineties, the Ministry of Defence believed that the Commander would see 20 years' service. Unfortunately, the Gulf War put paid to that idea. Not that the Commanders were found wanting - for exactly the opposite was the case - but that the harsh service conditions experienced in the aggressive and hostile deserts of the Middle East meant that the mid-life

In its first flush of youth the vehicle was called the Unipower 'Desert Commander' as in this Unipower brochure.

(brochure) **UNIPOWER** □ **Transporters**

Rapid deployment Tank/Heavy Equipment Transporter
The UNIPOWER Desert Commander rapid deployment Tank/Heavy Equipment Transporter is specifically designed for the role of heavy lift partner to the Challenger 2 Main Battle Tank and other tracked armoured vehicles.

Optimising fighting readiness
To safeguard a Main Battle Tank's fighting readiness and conserve fuel resources, it is essential to minimise non-combat track mileage. The force commander needs to be able to guarantee that armour is in the position where it is required - when required - fuelled, armed and ready to advance, with crews that are rested and fresh. Compliance with this necessitates heavy lift capability possessing swiftness and mobility over any surface, from asphalt to trackless desert. Such heavy lift capability must succeed in accomplishing its task when transporting up to 70 tonnes live combat weight of the latest generation of Main Battle Tank.

Performance
The capability designed into the UNIPOWER Desert Commander to meet these demands is not equalled by any vehicle in current service. Powered by a Cummins KTA3700 diesel producing 700 bhp at 2100 rpm, the Desert Commander's 8 x 8 tractor unit will sustain on-highway speeds in excess of 60 kph at gross combination weights of 115 tonne and over. Fully laden gradient performance includes climbing a continuous 21 percent incline and restarting on a gradient of 47 percent.

PROVEN RELIABILITY

When seen with the Nicolas six-axle trailer in place, the enormous length of the vehicle is apparent.

Shaun Connors

Twin Reynolds Boughton 25-tonne winches are fitted to assist with loading and unloading.

rebuild was required rather earlier than had originally been anticipated and it became obvious that the Commanders might not quite manage their 20 years.

In December 1998, John Spellar, the then Parliamentary Under-Secretary for Defence, announced that the Ministry of Defence was actively seeking a new tank transporter - or heavy equipment transporter (HET) as it had become fashionable to term such a vehicle. This, perhaps was not a surprise, but what was unexpected was that the Government stated that it was interested in industry bids to finance, supply, maintain and operate these tank transporters under the so-called 'private finance initiative' (PFI) scheme. We have become used to hearing about these PFI projects over the last few years, but the new tank transporter was to be a 'pathfinder' project - the first of the Government's PFI initiatives.

The new vehicle was to be rated at 75 tonnes, giving an all-up gross train weight approaching 115 tonnes. Despite this colossal payload, the loaded vehicle was expected to meet all European road-traffic legislation, particularly with respect to axle and wheel loadings - where overload can cause so much damage to old and vulnerable buildings, road surfaces and bridges - and engine emissions, where it was stated that the 'Euro 3' requirements were mandatory. The vehicle was expected not only to be able to carry the British Army's Challenger 2 tanks, but was also to be configured in such a way that it could carry other AFVs currently in service, such as the Warrior, FV432, and FV100 CVR(T) family, and other equipment such as engineer's plant, in an economical fashion. The anticipated in-service date was 2002, which really precluded designing a new vehicle from scratch.

The loaded MH8875 photographed during trials at Bagshot.

Four consortia were invited to bid. Each was required to develop and build the tractor and trailer, arrange the necessary finance to allow the Government to lease the equipment over a 20-year period, and provide logistical support. The consortia were Defence Heavy Transport, consisting of Serco and the German truck builder MAN; Fasttrax, made up of the American company Oshkosh with logistical support from Brown & Root; Hammer, which consisted of Foden Trucks, Broshuis Trailers and Lex Service; and Tactacon, a consortium of Alvis-Unipower - the successors to Scammell - with Ryder Defence and PHH Vehicle Management,

bank-rolled by independent merchant bankers Schroders. Defence Heavy Transport and Hammer were eliminated early on and by late 1999 it was a straight fight between the Oshkosh M1070F with a King trailer furnished by Fasttrax, and the Tactacon consortium's Alvis-Unipower MH8875 tractor with a French Nicolas trailer.

For a period, the Unipower team was confident that, not only was their vehicle superior to the M1070F, but that being British gave them an extra edge. The company was confident of receiving the contract, and it came as something of a blow in early 2001 when it was announced that Fasttrax was the preferred bidder. Unipower was eliminated from the competition, but the vehicle which they offered for the contract - the MH8875 - is worthy of closer study.

With a nod towards the Scammell's performance in the Gulf, the MH8875 was originally dubbed the 'Desert Commander' but was renamed to form an integral component of what was known as the Unipower M Series. Developed from the 8x8 bridge launch and delivery truck which the company had produced for the so-called BR90 programme ('bridging in the nineties') in the early 'nineties, the M Series was marketed as a range of high-performance, heavy-duty military vehicles.

The BR90 vehicles, which were the first of the range, were introduced in the eighties, but with the benefit of experience gained through the operation of the original (Scammell) Commander during the Gulf War in 1991, Unipower realised that the same chassis would lend itself to other applications, and was particularly suitable for use as a heavy equipment transporter. By 1993, the range consisted of five basic vehicles: a heavy recovery tractor, multi-role DROPS/PLS logistic support vehicle, bridge carrier/launcher, general-purpose chassis for cargo, tanker and other applications, and a heavy equipment transporter, which was being offered in 6x6 and 8x8 configurations. The vehicles shared a common design approach, with a powerful, usually Cummins, engine mounted behind a low-profile, space-frame forward-mounted cab. Drive was carried to all of the wheels through a ZF five-speed automatic transmission and transferred to the road via big, low-profile 24R21 on/off road radial tyres; inter-axle and cross-axle differential locks were fitted to ensure that the power was put where it was most needed.

In 1995, the Royal Army of Oman purchased nine 6x6 tractors with a payload rating of 60 tonnes. Designated the MH6660, this vehicle was designed to carry the Challenger 2 MBT and, although it did not comply with European axle-loading restrictions, this was hardly a consideration in the Kingdom of Oman. At the beginning of 1997 an 8x8 variant was developed which, in conjunction with a six-axle French-built Nicolas trailer, was able to meet the restrictions on axle loadings even when carrying a 75-tonne payload. The timing proved fortuitous, coinciding as it did with the MoD's requirement for a replacement for the Commander, and it was the combination of the 8x8 MH8875 tractor and Nicolas trailer which Alvis-Unipower pitched to the Ministry of Defence as part of the Tactacon 'tactical transport assets consortium'.

In contrast to the rather old-fashioned appearance of the Oshkosh tractor which was eventually selected by the MoD as the winner of the competition, the MH8875 was an impressive and handsome vehicle with a squat, modern profile and no-nonsense cab-forward stance which seemed to indicate the enormous power of the machine without having to resort to the apparent mass and bulk of its competitor. Where the tall, bonnetted Oshkosh harked back to the enormous tank transporters of WW2 and later, the low, purposeful MH8875 was obviously the result of some lateral thinking. It also had the benefit of being air-portable in the Lockheed C130 transport aircraft and was inside the NATO 'B envelope' for rail transfer.

Power was provided by a 19-litre six-cylinder Cummins turbo-charged diesel

Technical specification

Nomenclature: tractor, heavy equipment, 8x8, 75 tonne; Alvis-Unipower MH8875.

Engine: Cummins QSK-19-750; six cylinders; 19,000cc; turbo-charged, after-cooled diesel; overhead valves; power output, 750bhp at 1800-2150rpm; torque, 2275 lbf/ft at 1300rpm.

Transmission: ZF 5HP 1500 automatic; 5F1Rx2; inter-axle and cross-axle differential locks.

Suspension: live axles on semi-elliptical parabolic leaf springs.

Brakes: air-pressure dual circuit.

Construction: steel ladder chassis with steel space-frame cab.

Electrical system: 24V.

Dimensions (tractor only) Length, 395in. Width, 118in. Height, 133in (to top of cab-mounted exhaust). Wheelbase, 244in; bogie centres, front 67in, rear 60in. Weight, 46,200 lb.

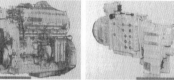

Brochure produced to sell both the MH6660 and the MH8875, together with the Tactacon presentation.

The Glory Days of Heavy Haulage

engine mounted in a full-width engine compartment behind the cab. The engine, reputedly derived from a unit designed by Cummins for diesel railcar applications, produced some 750bhp combined with a massive 1750 lbf/ft of torque; electronic management of the engine was controlled by a Cummins Quantum unit. Automatic transmission was fitted using a German-built ZF 5HP 1500 unit giving the vehicle five forward gears in combination with a three-phase integral torque converter and two-speed transfer case.

The transmission was controlled electronically by an EST 18M unit linked to the engine-management system for optimum gear changes regardless of load and road conditions. The drive was connected permanently to all eight wheels and the axles were of the spiral-bevel hub-reduction type; steering was provided on both front axles, which were 9.5-tonne units supplied by GKN, whilst the two rear axles were rated at 18 tonnes each and were manufactured by Unipower. The engine and transmission were chosen to provide a maximum road speed, loaded to 115 tonnes gross train weight, of more than 50mph. Unprepared wading depth was 48in.

The six-man, two-door crew-cab was a flat-floor, space-frame design with welded external panels; the driver was provided with a suspended seat and the remainder of the accommodation could be configured to provide seating for a co-driver and four-man tank crew, or as a sleeper cab for two. Heating equipment was fitted as standard, and air-conditioning was available, and the cab also included such features as observation hatch, anti-aircraft hip ring and gun mount. Although almost totally devoid of curves, the cab and engine compartment contributed in no small part to the purposeful appearance of the vehicle.

Twin independent Reynolds Boughton 25-tonne hydraulic winches were mounted behind the engine compartment to assist in loading and unloading disabled AFVs. The winches could be configured to pull in tandem or to allow one winch to pull an AFV down the trailer deck whilst the other is used to control the rate of descent.

A double-oscillating cast-steel fifth wheel was mounted

more-or-less above the centre-line of the third axle at a height of about 66 inches.

For the MoD trials the chosen trailer was a Nicolas TST 70MD 6/2 unit, with 24 independently-sprung wheels arranged on six axles, giving a maximum 12-tonne loading per axle. The rear three axles were designed to steer in response to inputs from the fifth-wheel coupling. The trailer was coupled to the tractor by means of an active gooseneck with hydraulic adjustment of height to give a levelling capability ranging from +22in to -18in and 15° vertical articulation on the move. The length of the trailer bed was chosen to allow the carriage of a single main battle tank, or two light tanks or infantry fighting vehicles (IFVs); loading was effected via a pair of hydraulically-operated ramps.

The vehicle was put through a series of reliability trials during 1998 and 1999, but was eventually eliminated in favour of the Oshkosh M1070F, a modified version of the standard US Army HET. One of the major reasons for the failure of the MH8875 was said to be its inability to comply with the Euro 3 emissions classification but it would seem unlikely that this was the sole reason.

However, the failure to secure this contract proved to be the last straw for Unipower and the company was put up for sale and wound up soon after. Sadly, Unipower and the link to Scammell has now disappeared, probably for good - the MH8875 prototype is reputedly lying in a semi-dismantled state at the former GKN works in Telford, now the home of Alvis Vehicles Limited, the engine and transmission having been returned to Cummins and ZF, respectively.

The truck is now believed to be with heavy haulage contractor ALE Ltd

The Glory Days of Heavy Haulage

Diamonds and rust

Like many, Pat Ware believes that the charismatic Diamond T Model 980/981 is the best-looking military vehicle ever produced – bar none!

IT'S incredible looking back, but in September 1939, the British Army was said to own just two heavy tank transporters with little prospect of supplies of adequate vehicles becoming available in a reasonable timescale. There were three reasons for this sorry state of affairs.

Firstly, the War Office had been slow to recognise that there was a need for such vehicles and when they finally got around to placing orders for the Scammell Pioneer, they found that Scammell's Watford factory was working flat out on producing artillery tractors. Secondly, although the Pioneer tank transporter had been already been uprated from 20 tons capacity to 30 tons, this was still not deemed adequate for the larger tanks that were on the drawing boards. Scammell made it clear to the War Office that the design, which dated from the early 'thirties, was not capable of further uprating without a significant re-design, for which there was no time. And, finally, there was no other British company capable of producing vehicles of this type.

The situation was hardly improved

following the evacuation from Dunkirk in May 1940, when so much equipment was left in France, and in an attempt to find a solution, the Ministry of Supply despatched a purchasing commission to the USA. The US Quarter Master Corps was asked to help locate suitable manufacturers for a wide range of trucks including a 40-ton tractor for the heavy tank-transporter role. Approaches were made to Mack, FWD, Ward La France, White... and Diamond T.

The Diamond T Motor Car Company of Chicago was already supplying a 4-ton 6x6 chassis (Models 967-975) to the Canadian Army for a variety of roles. This must have helped persuade the British Ministry of Supply (MoS) that, despite having no direct experience of building tank transporter tractors, the company had the necessary capability and, perhaps most importantly, it was determined that production could begin with the minimum of delay.

There followed a period of dithering while the War Office tried to decide whether to choose a tractor for semi-trailer, like the Scammell, or a ballast tractor for use with a full trailer. In the

end, the latter was felt to offer a better balance of operating characteristics, and in late 1940, the War Office prepared a specification for a tank-transporter train which comprised a 175-200bhp, diesel-powered tractor for use with a 40-ton multi-axle drawbar trailer. The specification stated explicitly that the vehicle was to incorporate 'proven components that were already in production' and that it was to be capable of carrying the English Mk 2 and Mk 4 tanks and the American M3 (without cupola). The laden height was not to exceed 150 inches and the loaded train was to be capable of negotiating a right-angled bend in a 28ft-wide road without reversing!

The point about using 'proven components' was well made for these were desperate times and there was no question of sufficient time being available to design and develop a vehicle from scratch. Without wishing to belittle the company's achievement, it seems that Diamond T took their commercial 12-ton Model 512, and drawing on experience gained in fulfilling the Canadian contracts, effectively jacked-up the chassis and slotted in a big Hercules DFXE diesel engine, Fuller transmission, and a new heavy-duty rear bogie employing Timken axles.

There was, however, one strange omission from the specification. It was stated quite explicitly that the tractor was for use only on metalled roads. Although the Scammell Pioneer was similarly not provided with a driven front axle, and was also for 'on-road use only', the tractor-and-semi-trailer layout did provide better performance in soft going and when

The classic closed-cab Diamond T Model 980 - this was probably one of the very first (of 394) vehicles supplied to the Ministry of Supply under the initial contract (SM2059). The wooden tool box on the front edge of the ballast box was omitted on later contracts.

The Glory Days of Heavy Haulage

This vehicle was also supplied under contract SM2059, but note the typical 'Micky Mouse ears' camouflage pattern, and carriers for petrol, oil and water fitted to the ballast box.

comparing the performance of the Diamond T with the Scammell, contemporary reports often stated that the American truck was easily defeated by a build-up of soil in front of the front wheels. With hindsight, it seems strange that the opportunity was not taken to specify a 6x6 configuration for the Diamond T.

By September 1941 the company had produced an engineering prototype for assessment and approval by the Inspection Board of the UK and Canada. All things considered, the company had done an excellent job in a remarkably short space of time and, with its stylish cab and long square bonnet, the resulting vehicle was not only extremely handsome but was also more than capable. In a press release produced at the time, the company stated proudly that 'these giant prime movers are the largest vehicles of their type ever built... (and will be) used with multiple wheeled trailers to provide fast transportation on highways for tanks of the largest size... and will also serve as recovery units for damaged tanks which are capable of repair'.

The first vehicle was almost certainly put through a series of rigorous trials at the US Army's Aberdeen Proving Ground facility in Maryland, but since deliveries were scheduled to begin in October 1941, scarcely a month after the first vehicle had been delivered, there was no time to incorporate any of the lessons that were learned during the trials. Similarly, one of the first trucks to be delivered to the UK was trialled by the Wheeled Vehicles Experimental Establishment (WVEE) but again, it must be remembered that production was already in full swing. It seems that the prototype was effectively the first production vehicle.

Production started in mid-1941 and continued until the end of the War.

The best estimate of the total number produced is 6554, of which 2095 were supplied to the UK under contract, with another 150 or so used vehicles supplied as ex-US Army surplus stock. The price for a Diamond T tractor purchased by the Ministry of Supply before the introduction of 'Lend-Lease' was £3250 - a considerable sum of money in 1941 and close to £100,000 in today's value. All British contracts for the Diamond T were placed by the MoS with the US Quarter Master Corps until August 1942, and subsequently with the Ordnance Board.

The company described the tractor as the Model 980, and this was subsequently joined by the Model 981 (see page 36). Under the US Army nomenclature scheme, the tractor was numbered 'M20' and the complete tractor-and-trailer combination was known as the 'M19'.

However, remember that the vehicle had originally been produced for use by the British Army, to a British specification and, although at the time the US Army had no other tank transporter, it was felt that the lack of front-wheel drive and the use of 'non-standard' diesel fuel mitigated against the truck and it was only somewhat-reluctantly adopted by the US

Open-cab Model 981 showing the winch fairlead rollers in the bumper and the re-positioned headlamps.

Technical specification

Nomenclature: tractor, 40 ton, 6x4, M20; Diamond T Model 980/981.

Engine: Hercules DFXE; six cylinders; 14,667cc; overhead valves; diesel; power output, 201bhp at 1800rpm; torque, 685 lbf/ft at 1150rpm.
Transmission: 4F1Rx3; 6x4.
Suspension: live axles on semi-elliptical leaf springs.
Brakes: air pressure.
Construction: steel ladder chassis with pressed-steel cab and rear body.
Electrical system: hybrid 6/12/24V (6V lighting, 12V charging, 24V starting).

Dimensions
Tractor only: length, 280in; width, 100in; height (to top of spare wheel in ballast box), 97in.
Complete train (according to trailer fitted): length, 645-696in; width, 114-120in; height (to top of spare wheel in ballast box), 97in. Wheelbase, 180in; bogie centres, 52in.
Weight: tractor only, 26,713 lb; gross train weight, 178,079 lb.

Army. The initial classification was 'substitute standard', and then, when supplies of the M26 'Dragon Wagon' got underway, it was downgraded to 'limited standard'.

Technical description
Though it may have been a tough, good-looking truck, the engine and transmission layout were totally conventional, and the Diamond T was no ground-breaker on the technical front.

In common with most of the American builders of larger trucks at that time, Diamond T had never produced their own engines and most of their pre-war offerings had been powered by proprietary Hercules petrol engines. However, for some reason the British War Office had been fixated on having diesel power for the tank-transporter role - perhaps it was felt this would allow the Diamond Ts to work more happily alongside the Gardner-powered Scammell Pioneers - so the power unit chosen for the Model 980 was the six-cylinder Hercules DFXE diesel, one of a series of related high-speed diesels offered by the Hercules Motors Company for military and commercial applications. Using Hercules' patented lateral combustion-chamber configuration, the DFXE produced 201bhp gross (178bhp net) from a capacity of 14.5 litres, with a massive 685 lbf/ft of torque. Huge in every sense

IWM, BU2043

Early closed-cab Model 980 with a Churchill tank load on the British Mk 2 trailer; photographed in Germany in March 1945.

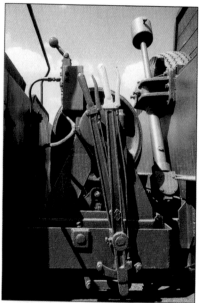

In 1943 the winch controls were moved out of the cab and placed beside the winch itself.

IWM, KID 3122

Rear view of the ballast box with the tailgate down; this vehicle has the 'petrol, oil and water' container inside the box. Note the white-painted differential to help convoy driving in blackout conditions.

of the word, the massive cast-iron lump weighed in at almost 25cwt, and effectively filled the lengthy under-bonnet space - on the right-hand side the view was dominated by triple oil filters whilst the left-hand side of the engine carried the injector pump and twin oil-bath air cleaners.

The engine was considered pretty reliable and could be kept running even when badly worn. Typical difficulties included valve-seat cracking, water-pump failure, and breakage of the injector-pump drive. Enthusiastic revving could also cause connecting-rod breakage and worn engines tended to become difficult to start when cold.

Diamond T

The Diamond T Motor Car Company was founded by Charles Arthur Tilt in Chicago in 1905, operating from a modest site on the north side of the city. Tilt started his manufacturing career building motor cars, although, in truth, like so many early manufacturers, he was simply bolting together proprietary components. But this allowed flexibility and there was no problem when, in 1911, a customer asked the company to construct a small truck. So successful was this venture, that within a few years, motor-car production had been abandoned altogether and Diamond T became one of the myriad of American custom truck builders.

During the Great War, the company was one of the suppliers of the Class B 'Liberty' trucks to the US Army, producing 638 examples in 1917-18. In 1916, the company had moved to a new 26-acre site on the south-west side of Chicago and that became the home of

Diamond T until the company ceased production under its own name in 1958.

In the early 'thirties, the company supplied a number of 1 and 1½ ton trucks to the US Army, but for most of its life the company tended to concentrate on the medium to heavy end of the market. Diamond T trucks were exported across the globe, and by 1930, the company was said to have distributors in 60 countries worldwide, including a UK office, firstly at Isleworth, Middlesex, and subsequently at Richmond in Surrey.

As for so many manufacturers, the outbreak of WW2 brought considerable prosperity, and although civilian models were produced alongside military vehicles during the early years of the War, by the spring of 1942 the company had turned over exclusively to war production, producing 50,000 military vehicles during the years 1940-45. During this time, the factory was often working 24 hours a day, seven days a week turning out the 4-ton 6x6 chassis

which was used for the Models 967-975, largely for the Canadian and American Armies, and the charismatic Model 980/981.

The immediate post-war years saw the company in real difficulties and although production continued fitfully through the 'fifties, in 1958 Diamond T was absorbed into the White empire. Production was moved to the Reo (Ransome E Olds) plant in Lansing, Michigan. In 1967, the trucks were re-named Diamond-Reo and in 1971 the company was sold to F L Cappaert. Although a few hundred trucks were produced by the new owners and subsequently by Consolidated International, and then Osterlund, by 1996 Diamond T trucks seemed to have disappeared for good.

And the origin of that wonderful name? There's no mystery about it and it certainly didn't require a focus group - the 'Diamond' simply stood for quality - the 'T' stood for Tilt.

Rear view with the ballast box closed.

Tank Museum

The prodigious power output of the big Hercules was fed through an 11in-diameter twin-plate Lipe clutch to the four-speed Fuller gearbox, in unit construction with the engine. A short drive shaft connected the main gearbox to a three-speed (normal, low and high) auxiliary unit, also of Fuller manufacture. The combination of the two gearboxes provided 12 speeds forward and three in reverse. You could be forgiven for thinking that, in combination with the powerful diesel engine, this was probably more than sufficient to allow the truck to cope with most road and load conditions, but where it was difficult to gain sufficient traction, perhaps due to low adhesion caused by snow or ice, or, when called upon to move excess weight, Diamond Ts were frequently double- or even triple-headed.

Ponder the sight - and sound - of that for a moment!

In combination with the 12-speed transmission, the Hercules engine was able to provide a road speed - remember, this was not intended as an off-road vehicle - of 23-25mph loaded. This was pretty impressive at a time when the equivalent Scammell was scarcely capable of 15mph, but a major criticism of the vehicle was that the gear ratios were all wrong and that it required a skilled driver to get the best out of the engine - a gearchange was required at exactly the moment that the engine was producing its peak power. A good driver could compensate for this by juggling gears between the main and auxiliary boxes but this practice of 'split changing' was not easy to do without damaging the selector forks or gear wheels, and sometimes required input from both the driver and mate!

The undriven Timken front axle was suspended on huge 13-leaf semi-elliptical springs which were an impressive six inches deep at the U-bolts. At the rear, there was a pair of Timken SD462W double-reduction axles assembled into a driving bogie, also suspended on massive, semi-elliptical springs, this time, inverted. Axle location was controlled by six rubber-bushed torque rods, two above the axles, and four below. Another criticism of the Diamond T was that inadequate lubrication of the bogie pivots could cause the whole assembly to break away under starting load due to stress cracks forming around the seized bushes.

Directional control was provided by Ross variable ratio cam-and-roller steering gear, without power assistance. The driver was only saved from developing biceps like Mike Tyson by virtue of the fact that

the steering wheel was 22 inches in diameter, giving considerable leverage. The stopping department was no less impressive and the 17.5in drums were four inches wide at the front - compare this with the Scammell's complete lack of front-wheel brakes - and four-and-a-half inches at the rear.

This impressive array of automotive equipment was attached to a heat-treated manganese steel chassis, no less than 10.5 inches deep. The parallel chassis rails were held apart by seven riveted cross-members and a huge front bumper; a towing pintle was carried on the front and rear-most cross-members.

The driver and mate were accommodated in an attractive 'art deco' styled, albeit rather narrow, enclosed two-door cab, mated to a long 'coffin' nose which terminated in an upright cast radiator; the front wheels were covered by huge semi-circular wings, cut short at the front to clear the bumper. By virtue of having simply been borrowed from the company's civilian trucks, the original cab was outrageously styled for a military

vehicle, and it is almost impossible not to mention the 30° 'V' shaped windscreen, the swoopy styling of the instrument panel, and the idiosyncratic cab-roof ventilator which perches jauntily over the apex of the screen. But where many

IWM, H28811

Photographed during trailer trials, this is an early Model 980 coupled to a Shelvoke & Drewry Mk 2 trailer.

The open cab, adopted in August 1943, really spoilt the truck's appearance. This is a Model 981, again coupled to a British Mk 2 trailer; note the typical 'bivouac' constructed over the ballast body to provide overnight accommodation for the crew.

trucks of the period were less than successful in marrying a civilian cab with the no-nonsense military wings and bonnets, the Diamond T manages to pull-off this trick with great aplomb and the result has incredible presence and confidence.

The rear body consisted simply of a large, flat-sided steel ballast box, built by Gar Wood Industries, which was designed to carry up to about 15,000 lb in cast-iron weights in a central, open area, to provide sufficient traction for the rear wheels. The body also included stowage compartments for tools and equipment and for the spare wheel. A canvas or steel-roofed enclosure was often constructed over the ballast box by British tank-transporter crews to provide make-shift overnight accommodation during the long 'lifts', or 'drags', as the operations were called. During the post-war years these enclosures became increasingly sophisticated, often being provided with timber bulkheads and hinged access doors... but, nevertheless, a far cry from the purpose-made bunks provided in the

Open cab with the canvas erected.

cab of the current British Army Scammell Commander tank transporter.

Winch power

A horizontal-spindle Gar Wood 40-ton winch was installed between the cab and the ballast box, and was chain-driven from a power take-off on the auxiliary gearbox. Fairlead rollers were fitted above the rear-most chassis cross-member to allow disabled AFVs to be loaded using winch power. The controls were originally placed inside the cab itself, but this made it difficult for the winch operator to monitor progress during loading and unloading without the assistance of another crew member, and, as recounted below, they were subsequently moved to the operator's platform beside the winch itself.

As delivered, the winch had no paying-on gear and the resulting bunching and snagging of the cable under load had a bad effect on cable life. In 1944, the British developed a pendulum-operated paying-on and tensioning device with which most British Diamond Ts were retro-fitted. This effectively solved the problem.

Where the original vehicle was configured only for winching from the rear, in late 1942 or early 1943, the US Army specified a recovery - or 'tank retriever' - variant of the tractor which was designated 'Model 981'. It actually differed very little from its predecessor and is easily recognised by the winch fairlead rollers fitted into the left-hand side of the, not insubstantial, front bumper which allowed winching to take place from a forward position. To assist in this task, the winch was provided with 500 feet of rope in place of the 980's 300 feet.

Open cab and changes to winch controls

Aside from the introduction of the Model 981, the only other major modification was the adoption of the standard open

Although it was described as a 'tank transporter', the Diamond T was often called upon to carry other loads. This is an LCVP amphibious assault craft being carried on a modified 45-ton Rogers trailer during the advance into Germany in 1945.

Above: Nice overhead view of what is said to be the prototype vehicle in ex-works condition; note the side-marker reflector on the ballast box.

Right: A 40-ton Gar Wood model 5M723B chain-driven winch was mounted between the cab and the ballast box.

cab and folding windscreen in August 1943. This was introduced across almost the entire range of US-built military vehicles in an attempt to minimise unnecessary consumption of materials and to reduce the shipping height of vehicles.

The new cab did have an unexpected bonus in being appreciably wider and thus providing room for three up front against the original two-seater. However, although the always-impressive 'coffin' nose remained, many believe that the Diamond T lost most of its good looks with the adoption of the open cab.

At around the same time that the open cab was adopted, the winch controls were also moved outside the cab and were placed alongside the winch itself.

Trailers

Although Scammell had been keen to

supply the trailers, and had actually prepared a design, it was decided that the tractor would be used with a 40-ton, three-axle, 24-wheeled trailer which had been developed by the British company Cranes of Dereham. A prototype trailer was produced by Cranes and delivered in May 1941, by which time the decision had already been taken to also purchase

a trailer from Rogers in the USA - very close to the Cranes design, but rated at 45 (short) tons.

In fact, the trailers produced for the first contract for 485 Diamond T tractors were split between Cranes and Rogers, with 200 coming from the British company and 285 from the USA. But, as it happened, only 89 of these 200 trailers - subsequently described as the Mk 1 or 'Cranes design' - were constructed by Cranes before the Ministry of Supply decided that the company would be better employed using its limited production capacity to construct lighter trailers, and it was decided that all future production would come from the USA. Alongside Rogers, other American companies involved in producing what was known as

The winch fairlead rollers in the front bumper identify this as a Model 981, and it is another of the vehicles supplied under the first Ministry of Supply contract; the photograph was taken during recovery exercises in the UK.

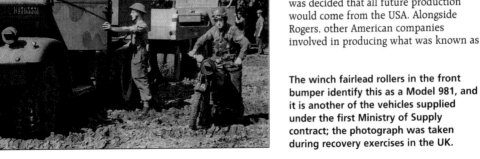

Standard front three-quarter view of the Model 981. Note the single headlamp with its blackout mask and the typical British sidelights on the wings (as well as the marker lights on the bumper apron).

The right-hand under-bonnet view is dominated by three oil filters mounted side-by-side.

Rear view showing the massive towing pintle and rollers for the winch cable.

the M9 45-ton trailer, included Checker Cab, Pointer-Williamette, Winter-Weiss, and Fruehauf.

One of the major differences between the British trailers and the Rogers was in the wheel and tyre equipment - the Cranes employed a 6.00x20in tyre, whilst the Rogers used an 8.25x15in. It's worth noting that, despite their existence in larger numbers, many British tank-transporter crews hated the Rogers (and other American) trailers with a passion, believing that the brakes were far less effective, and that the smaller wheels led to over-loading of the tyres which, in turn, caused more frequent blow-outs... and just to make matters worse, the wheel studs were prone to shearing-off making the task of changing wheels and tyres even more unpleasant and time-consuming.

Although Cranes made no more 40-ton trailers during WW2, the MoS did not stick to its plan for allocating the production exclusively to the 'States and the British companies Scottish Motor Traction (SMT), R A Dyson, Shelvoke & Drewry, Hands Trailers, and the British Trailer Company also produced a version of the Mk 1 trailer. Dyson re-designed the trailer, providing adjustable guide rails on the inner edges of the trackways and omitting the outer guide rails which were used on the Mk 1. These changes provided the trailer with increased utility, allowing it to carry AFVs of differing widths. This design was also produced by SMT, Hands Trailers, and the British Trailer Company - and was known as the Mk 2 or 'Dyson' design.

During their post-war British service, the Diamond Ts were also used with the Cranes-designed 50-ton FV3601 trailer which was produced by both Cranes and Dyson through three 'marks'.

Deployment by all of the Allies

The Diamond T was used by all of the Allies with supplies going to the US Army, Britain, Russia and Canada and it was used in all of the WW2 theatres. A handful were also supplied to the Free Poles and the Czechs.

Although it was intended primarily for use as a carrier of tanks and self-propelled guns, with the trackways, stops and guides of the trailer designed especially for this purpose, it was not long before the invading army in Europe realised that the Diamond T and trailer could also be used in the role of what, today, we would call a heavy equipment transporter. Sometimes this required some modification to the trailer but photographs and documentary evidence indicate that the Diamond T was used as

Photographed at the Durham Light Infantry Museum, this is an early closed-cab Model 980. The headlights were re-positioned on the front bumper apron by the British Army during the post-war years.

Des Penny

The Glory Days of Heavy Haulage

◀ About one (open-cabbed) vehicle in nine was fitted with the M49 anti-aircraft machine-gun mount and hip ring mounted on steel legs above the passenger seat.

In the post-war years, the Diamond T ▶ was the mainstay of the tank transporter fleet of many European Armies. This example has been fitted with additional indicator and marker lights and new headlamps in an effort to make it visible to modern traffic.

In the mid-fifties the British Army replaced the original Hercules engine with a Rolls-Royce C6NFL-143 unit - this necessitated changes to the bonnet sides to accommodate the air cleaners. ▼

a transporter for gun tractors, landing craft and landing vehicles, assault boats, amphibious vehicles, and bulk ammunition.

In the months following D-Day, British Diamond Ts attached to 21 Army Group carried out no less than 8266 operational moves of AFVs in the drive across Europe, amounting to a total movement of one-and-a-half million vehicle miles. The largest operation took place in March 1945 when 383 transporters from, inter alia, 15, 451 and 545 Tank Transporter Companies moved 361 Comet and Stuart tanks belonging to 11th Armoured Division from the Diest area to Wesel following Monty's successful 'Operation Plunder' crossing of the Rhine.

After the War, the Diamond T became Britain's primary heavy tank transporter until it was replaced by the Thornycroft Antar Mk 2 and Mk 3 tractors in the 'fifties, but even then, large numbers of Diamond Ts were held in 'war reserve' stocks as well as being allocated to the UK-based tank-transporter units. In 1954, 700 of the 1000 British tank transporters were Diamond Ts.

In fact, so important was the Diamond

T to the British tank-transporter role that in 1956, many of the remaining Diamond T tractors were fitted with Rolls-Royce C6NFL-143 diesel engines in place of the aging Hercules units. This gave them a new lease of life and, coincidentally, provided a more useful power band which, despite the nominal output of the engine actually being lower, gave an additional turn of speed and allowed the vehicle to be uprated to 50 tons.

War-surplus, ex-US Army vehicles were also supplied to Israel, Australia, France, Denmark, Italy and other European countries as part of the post-war Marshall Aid plan and many of these remained in service for a further three decades. Similarly, many surplus military vehicles found employment with heavy-haulage companies in the 'fifties and 'sixties.

Today, despite its size, ponderous speed, and prodigious thirst, the Diamond T remains a firm favourite with collectors and a well-turned out tractor, particularly with the bonnet raised, will always attract an admiring crowd at a show.

Further reading

Diamond T 980/981: the M19 tank-transporter train in British Army service. Ware, Pat. Croydon, Warehouse Publications, 2001. ISBN 1-903062-02-0.

Diamond T tank transporters: the 980/981 tractor unit and its American and British trailers. Vanderveen, B H. London, Wheels & Tracks 55, 1996. ISSN 0263-7081.

Diamond T type 980/981. Freathy, Les and Robin Pearson. Wellington, Roundoak Publishing, 2001. ISBN 1-871565-36-7.

If one Diamond T was not sufficient, it was permissible to double- or even triple-head to deal with an abnormal load. The load in this case is the 78-ton A39 Tortoise heavy assault tank being carried on the 70/80-ton five-axle trailer.

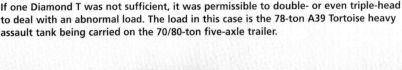

ANTAR
POET WARRIOR

Despite its civilian origins, the Antar Mk 1 established Thornycroft as the major supplier of tank-transporter tractors to the British Army for more than 30 years

During WW2, the British Army suffered from having a myriad of different vehicle types in service, but at the time there was little choice. At the end of the War, a serious attempt was made to rationalise those vehicles which were to remain on the inventory into the post-war period and all sorts of non-standard and 'scarcely-adequate' vehicles were disposed of. On the tank-transporter front, there was seen to be no future need for the medium tank transporters such as the White, the White-Ruxtall and the smaller Macks and they were put up for sale. Of the heavier tank transporters, the 6x4 Albion CX24S had already been demoted to engineering duties and some of the 20-ton Scammell Pioneers were similarly converted. This left the RASC with the 30-ton Pioneer, together with its dedicated semi-trailer, and the American Diamond T Models 980 and 981, with the 40/45-ton Cranes, Dyson and Rogers draw-bar trailers.

However, all was not well...

Whilst the larger Allied tanks of WW2 had posed some transportation difficulties, the Diamond T seemed able to cope with weights up to 45 tons, but

the development of the huge Russian Joseph Stalin 3 (JS3) main battle tank and the need for the Allies to design a counterpart, inevitably meant that tanks were going to get bigger still. The Scammell was thus of restricted utility, and even the Diamond T occasionally had to be double-headed to deal with such monsters as the German King Tiger and the A39 Tortoise heavy assault tank, both of which weighed in at somewhat more than the Diamond T's nominal 40/45-ton rating. Although the 78-ton Tortoise was quickly abandoned as impractical, Britain's standard post-war 'heavy gun' tank was intended to be the FV214 Conqueror, and with an all-up battle weight of 66 tons, this too was theoretically well beyond the capability of the Diamond T.

As part of the post-war military-vehicles development programme the Fighting Vehicles Research and Development Establishment (FVRDE) had designed two tractors which were intended to solve the problem of shifting these, seemingly, ever-growing tanks - the 60-ton FV1000 and the 30-ton FV1200.

Although prototypes of both machines were produced and trialled, both projects were running late and found themselves in considerable difficulties - and as it happened, both were ultimately abandoned as unrealistic.

By 1950, the War Office was in the unenviable position of having ordered quantities of the new Conqueror tank, and of the 50-ton Dyson trailer required to move them, but of having no suitable prime mover. As it happened, the ageing Diamond T was probably more than up to the job but nobody was really happy about it and the War Office was casting around for a solution.

'And then a miracle happened...'

The Basingstoke-based company, Transport Equipment (Thornycroft), had been quietly working away with the civil-engineering contractors George Wimpey and Sons, on a large prime mover for transporting steel oil pipelines across the deserts of Iraq. Whilst FVRDE and the War Office had been dithering about a suitable replacement for the Diamond T, it had taken the Thornycroft engineering team just 10 months to design the truck from scratch and

Below: One of the original Mighty Antar oilfield tractors with a 50-ton forward-loading semi-trailer. This trailer was used during the initial trials.

build the first vehicle! Dubbed Mighty Antar, after the Arabian poet warrior Antar Ibn Shadded, who was famed for his powers of strength and endurance, Thornycroft's new baby was positively heaped with superlatives by the technical press. It was described as the 'largest vehicle produced in Britain' and was apparently 'an unparalleled achievement in British heavy commercial transport'.

Of course, the War Office had been keeping an eye on what was going on, and was certainly present at the vehicle's press launch in February 1950. Indeed, it could hardly have missed it for the launch was held on the FVRDE test site at Bagshot. A total of 35 of these Rover Meteorite-powered Antars was constructed and delivered to the Iraq Petroleum Company where, for almost 24 hours a day each carried 65 ton loads of steel pipe across the merciless desert, clocking up a total of three-quarters of a million miles of service.

Technical specification

Nomenclature: tractor, 30 ton, GS, permanent body, 6x4; FV12001; Thornycroft Antar.

Engine: Rover Meteorite Mk 204; eight cylinders in V formation; 18,012cc; overhead valves; power output 260bhp at 2000rpm.
Transmission: 6F1Rx3.
Suspension: live axles on semi-elliptical springs.
Brakes: air pressure.
Construction: steel ladder chassis with steel-panelled cab and steel ballast body.
Electrical system: 24V.

Dimensions
Length, 332in; width, 111in; height, 120in.
Wheelbase, 185 + 62in.
Weight, 44,220 lb.

However, there was no question that this was anything other than a commercial vehicle and Thornycroft had apparently not even considered that there might be a military application for the Antar. But perhaps the War Office had done more than simply keep its eyes open, for in August 1949 the Director of Fighting Vehicle Production had reported at a 'B Vehicles' development meeting that there was 'a vehicle being developed by Thornycrofts... called the Mighty Antar, which should tow an 82-ton load.' The Deputy Director of Weapons Development expressed a keen interest in the vehicle, pointing out that it could provide the solution to the problem of replacing the Diamond T whilst development of the FV1000 and FV1200 projects continued. It was agreed that the availability and suitability of the Antar should be investigated during 1951/52. However, within less than 12 months of this meeting, Thornycroft pre-empted the War Office and launched the vehicle.

The War Office must have been more than impressed with its capabilities. Without even waiting for a development vehicle to be constructed, in 1951 the Ministry of Supply placed a contract (6/Veh/5302) with Thornycroft for 15 steel-bodied Antar tractors for use with the FV3601 Dyson 50-ton drawbar trailer;

This page: The first military Antar to be completed was registered 02BD15. It was delivered to FVRDE on 27 June 1951, and was put through the normal 'automotive and reliability' trial programme; at this stage, the winch was not fitted but a ballasted wooden box was put in its place on the right-hand side behind the cab. Notice how similar the truck is in general concept to the Diamond T Model 980/981.

registration numbers were 02BD15-02BD20, and 12BD74-12BD82. The first chassis was laid down in Thornycroft's Basingstoke factory on 20 March 1951 and the completed vehicle was delivered to FVRDE for testing on 27 June, albeit without its winch. The tractors were priced at £14,100 each, giving a total contract value of around £211,500 (1951 prices). A second batch of eight Mk 1 steel-bodied Antars was ordered for the RAF in 1955 (contract 6/Veh/5718 - registrations 47AN03-47AN10).

Where the civilian Antars had been powered by a diesel version of the Rolls-Royce designed Rover Meteorite V8 engine, the military version was

Left and above: The second production vehicle (02BD16) has been preserved in the REME/SEME historic vehicles collection and is seen here both in service and on the rally field. There are various small differences when compared to the first example, most notably the depth of the ballast box.

equipped with a petrol-fired version of the same power unit. Apparently, FVRDE had felt that the diesel was underpowered, and anyway, was also at

some pains to point out that the Mk 204 Meteorite provided some commonality of design, and hence a small simplification in parts supply, with the V12 Meteor which had been specified for use in the Conqueror and Centurion tanks which it was likely to find itself carrying. However, many felt that the use of a petrol engine, consuming fuel at a terrifying rate when worked hard, was a retrograde step when

both the Scammell Pioneer and the Diamond T had been diesel powered. It was not until the deliveries of the Mk 3/Mk 3A Antar that the supporters of diesel power got their way.

Despite not having originated from FVRDE, the Antars were assigned the number FV12001, which showed that they were considered to be related to the FV1200 series which was still under development. At the time, Britain's tank transporter fleet was numbered close to 1000 (contrast this with today's figure of around 120), and the small quantity ordered suggests that the Antar was either seen simply as a stopgap measure, for which remember the MoS had carried no development costs, or as a development vehicle.

Further information

We would like to thank the Thornycroft Society, and particularly Chris Tree, for supplying some of the photographs which illustrate this article. If you are interested in joining the Society, contact the Membership Secretary Mervyn Annetts, at The New Coach House, Innersdown, Micheldever, Winchester, Hampshire SO21 3BW, (tel 01962 774574).

If you want to learn more about Thornycroft, look for copies of the following long out-of-print books:

Breakdown: A History Of Recovery Vehicles In The British Army.
Baxter, Brian S.
London, HMSO, 1989.
ISBN 0-11-290456-4.

Illustrated History Of Thornycroft Trucks And Buses.
Baldwin, Nick.
Sparkford, Haynes Publishing Group, 1989.
ISBN 0-85429-707-3.

Above and below: Good front and rear views of RAF tractors 47AN09 (without its winch) and 47AN10. Compare the rear view to that of the first War Office tractor which had not been fitted with the winch fairlead rollers.

The first production vehicle, registered 02BD15, was put through the normal FVRDE 'automotive and reliability' trial programme and a number of small problems came to light during the course of these trials. There were technical difficulties with the engine which necessitated a rebuild halfway through the trial, and continual problems in the driveline, which was over-stressed by the 260bhp produced by the engine. However,

Above: The Mk 1 military Antar was derived from the civilian machine developed on behalf of civil engineering contractors Geo Wimpey. Photographed in March 1950, amidst much excitement on the road, this vehicle is en-route to the Lebanon.

Below and right: Antars under production and lined up outside Thornycroft's Basingstoke works; the external photograph shows seven of the eight Mk 1 tractors manufactured for the RAF in 1955.

production was not halted during the trials programme so there was no opportunity to even begin to correct any design problems until the Mk 2 tractors were ordered in 1952. In fact, the transmission problems were never fully resolved. When worked a little too hard, even the Mk 3/Mk 3A Antars were prone to overheating their rear-axle oil and destroying the transfer case in spectacular fashion, dumping the gears, bearings and smashed pieces of casing and drive-shaft onto the road in a great pool of dirty oil - I understand they were particularly prone to doing this when climbing the hill on the autobahn outside the Fallingbostel barracks.

Although it would be difficult to call the truck handsome, there is no doubt that it was an enormous and impressive machine by the standards of

Right: Fourth tractor from the War Office contract - registered 02BD18.

the day. With its huge blunt nose covering twin radiators, massive wheels and perpendicular cab design, it certainly had a significant presence on the road. The general chassis layout followed that of the Diamond T, with a front-mounted engine, chain-driven winch sited behind the cab, twin rear wheels, and a steel ballast body designed to accommodate up to 15 tons of cast-iron

weights - it even shared the handrail design around the edges of the ballast box with the Diamond T. For some reason, the first vehicle had no rear mudguards and was also fitted with a deeper ballast body than the others, but otherwise, there were no significant differences between the 15 vehicles.

The first production vehicle (02BD15) remained at FVRDE, Chertsey until February 1961 where it was used as a general prime mover; similarly, RAF tractor 47AN03 (although it was re-registered 75ZB93, then RGX 978, then 60EP57) also ended up at Chertsey. However, most Antars spent their working lives with BAOR in Germany, based either at Sennelager or Fallingbostel. When the ballast tractor and draw-bar trailer concept fell from favour during the 'fifties, the vehicles probably found themselves being used either as 'shunters' or recovery tractors.

By 1952 Thornycroft had started work on the first of the Mk 1B or Mk 2 Antars, the FV12002 fifth-wheel tractor. This in turn led to a timber-bodied ballast tractor (FV12003) and then, in 1958, to the diesel-engined Mk 3 Antar, produced as a fifth-wheel tractor for use with a semi-trailer (FV12004) and as a ballast-bodied conversion (FV12006) for support and recovery duties.

Thornycroft ANTAR Mk 2

Having just looked at the Thornycroft Antar Mk 1 tank transporter tractors, now we turn the spotlight on the Mk2, which was produced both as a ballast tractor and a tractor for semi-trailer

During WW2 the British Army was equipped with three basic types of tank transporter. The early rigid-chassis vehicles such as the American Mack, White-Ruxtall and White trucks had started to enter service in 1940. By 1942, the Diamond T Model 980/981 ballast tractors were being received from the USA for use with a full trailer. And alongside the Albion and Scammell tractor/semi-trailer combinations there was a semi-trailer conversion of the Diamond T.

Despite being used in the Middle East and in France in 1940, the rigid-chassis vehicles, which were rated at just 18 tons, had quickly proved themselves less than adequate for the increasingly-heavy AFVs, and were soon abandoned, but the other machines remained in

service in all of the WW2 theatres. At the end of the War, the Diamond T ballast tractors (with various American and British 45- and 50-ton trailers) and the Scammell Pioneer and Diamond T tractor/semi-trailer outfits remained on strength but were obviously not getting any younger and the War Office was keen to find a replacement. In 1951, almost as an experiment, the Army had taken delivery of 15 examples - plus eight subsequently supplied to the Air Ministry - of a steel-bodied ballast tractor derived from the commercial Thornycroft Mighty Antar. Finding that this provided a satisfactory replacement for the ageing Diamond T, the Fighting Vehicles Research and Development Executive (FVRDE) drew up a specification for a militarised Mk 2 variant.

For the Mk 2 Antar, the Army decided that both ballast-bodied and fifth-wheel variants were required. However, there was no 'development' of the military Antar in the normally-accepted sense of the word and certainly no development contract. On 16 April 1952, under contract number 6/Veh/7360, Thornycroft simply began work on Antar chassis number 54768 working to FVRDE Specification 9042. This was the first of a batch of 57 FV12002 60-ton tractors which ultimately included both fifth-wheel tractors and those with a ballast body (see below).

Strangely, the first chassis, along with the next down the line, was despatched to South Africa (which at that time was still under British control), but on 8 October 1952 the British Army took delivery of its first Mk 2 Antar - chassis number 54770, registered with census number 94BD75. Of course, the major difference between the first Mk 2 and the Mk 1 was that a Davies 'Magnet' fifth-wheel coupling, with a 34-ton capacity, was now bolted across the chassis in place of the steel ballast body. But in truth, little else was changed.

Like the Mk 1, the massive bonnet was

photographs: Thornycroft Society

Above: FV12002 complete with the FV3001 60-ton semi-trailer posing outside the Thornycroft works.

Left: Superb overhead view of the FV12002 fifth-wheel tractor showing the winch and fifth wheel.

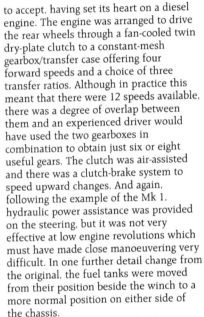

fronted by twin radiators giving the vehicle a huge, bluff appearance - the 'Antar' name was displayed across the radiators using Thornycroft's distinctive 'T' as the centre. Power was still provided by the huge, and thirsty, petrol-fired Rover Meteorite engine in carburetted Mk 204 form - which the Army was still reluctant

One of the last petrol-engined Antars in British Army service seen here with the FV3001 60-ton trailer.

to accept, having set its heart on a diesel engine. The engine was arranged to drive the rear wheels through a fan-cooled twin dry-plate clutch to a constant-mesh gearbox/transfer case offering four forward speeds and a choice of three transfer ratios. Although in practice this meant that there were 12 speeds available, there was a degree of overlap between them and an experienced driver would have used the two gearboxes in combination to obtain just six or eight useful gears. The clutch was air-assisted and there was a clutch-brake system to speed upward changes. And again, following the example of the Mk 1, hydraulic power assistance was provided on the steering, but it was not very effective at low engine revolutions which must have made close manoeuvering very difficult. In one further detail change from the original, the fuel tanks were moved from their position beside the winch to a more normal position on either side of the chassis.

The enclosed insulated cab, which was derived from the Comjoints-designed unit fitted to the original Iraq Petroleum Company Antars, was also virtually unaltered from the Mk 1 machine. At first, the cabs were supplied by Bonallack but late models were constructed by Thornycroft using panels supplied by Motor Panels of Coventry. Accommodation was provided for a three-man crew, with

an anti-aircraft gunner's observation hatch in the roof above the passenger's seat. Finally, there was a bit of fiddling with the headlamps, which on vehicles supplied under later contracts, were now twinned and placed below the front bumper. Early vehicles were fitted with large semaphore turn signals on extended brackets behind the cab doors but these were later replaced with amber flashing indicators.

A 20-ton Darlington type 70/31 chain-driven winch, carrying 350 feet of 7/8in steel rope, was fitted across the chassis behind the cab and was driven through a power take-off on the main gearbox. The winch was intended to assist in loading disabled AFVs and there was no provision for operation from the front.

photograph: Richard Grevatte-Ball

The Glory Days of Heavy Haulage

Left and below: FV12003 ballast-bodies tractor under test at FVRDE. Note the lifting rings on the wheels.

Above: Huge rear spring and typical earth-mover tread tyres.

Below: View of the winch drum.

Where the original Mk 1 ballast-bodied tractors had been intended as little more than an experiment to supplement the ageing Diamond Ts, the fifth-wheel variant was clearly meant as a replacement for the by-now archaic Scammell Pioneers. Rated at just 30 tons, even during WW2 the Pioneer had been inadequate and was certainly not up to the task of carrying the increasingly-heavy AFVs coming into service at that time. The fifth-wheel Antar was nominally rated at 60 tons and contemporary documentation stated that the vehicle was able to operate at gross train weights of 140 tons. It was intended to be used with either the Sankey FV3001 (later superseded by the very similar FV3005) 60-ton semi-trailer or the FV3011 50-ton semi-trailer produced by Joseph Sankey, Taskers of Andover, or GKN.

Along with its purpose-built Sankey semi-trailer, the Mk 2 Antar was announced in the May 1954 issue of 'Soldier' magazine. The author of the piece made much of the size of the vehicle and the skill required to operate it. And, although at the time the Antar was restricted to a maximum speed of 12mph on British roads, 'Soldier' was also keen to point out that it was actually capable of a dizzying 28mph 'in an emergency'.

At more or less the same time, production also began of a Mk 2 ballast-bodied variant (FV12003) initially rated at 50 tons; it was very similar to the Mk 1 machine but for some reason the decision was taken to use the standard Thornycroft ballast body, which was of composite steel and timber, rather than using the all-steel construction of the Mk 1. The body

included a small steel access ladder at the rear, and there was a stowage position at the very back for a spare wheel - on the fifth-wheel tractors the spare wheel was carried on the trailer swan-neck. The change from the steel to timber ballast body also reduced the capacity by 18% and the Mk 2 was able to carry no more than 16 ½ tons of ballast compared to 20 tons for the Mk 1.

Although the advantage of the ballast-bodied vehicles is that they can be used both as 'first aid' recovery tractors as well as hauling a tank on a full trailer, it seems that this vehicle was initially seen only as an interim requirement. Contemporary paperwork states that the vehicle was fitted with a 'removable' ballast body and there are occasional references in print to the ballast body being 'temporary' - indeed, in Thornycroft's provisional User Handbook produced for the RAF, it is stated quite explicitly that 'these vehicles are fitted with a ballast body... as a temporary measure, and will ultimately be

FV12002 fifth-wheel tractor and FV3011 50-ton semi-trailer carrying an unusual load - an American-built M107 175mm self-propelled gun.

equipped with a semi-trailer attachment'.

It was certainly easy enough to convert the vehicle from one configuration to the other and back again, and perhaps it was originally planned that the Antars would eventually be used only with semi-trailers, and that the (soon to be) up-engined Diamond Ts (or some other as-yet unavailable vehicle) would be used with the FV3601 Cranes and Dyson 50-ton draw-bar trailers. However, this did not happen and the two variants saw service alongside one another for the entire life of the Mk 2.

Despite some weakness in the transmission which occasionally led to catastrophic failure under load, the Antar proved itself to be a reliable piece of kit... but nevertheless, the Army's dissatisfaction with the power unit remained and it was hoped that by 1954 a suitable diesel engine might be available.

Engine trials
The Diamond T remained in service for most of the life of the Antar (regardless of 'mark'), and this, of course, was diesel-powered. So too, was the Gardner-engined Scammell Pioneer.

For various reasons, the Army had really wanted a diesel in the Antar but were never able to find an engine which provided sufficient power. In the specification for the FV12002, FVRDE stated quite categorically, in at least two separate sections, that 'until a suitable compression-ignition power unit has been approved for use with this vehicle, propulsion shall be by means of a Meteorite... petrol engine'.

Keen to find a solution to the problem of diesel power for the Antar, between March and October 1956 a standard (petrol) Meteorite-powered FV12002 was pitched head-to-head against a couple of experimental vehicles - an FV12002 fitted with a supercharged Rolls-Royce C6SFL diesel, and an FV12003 which was equipped with an experimental high-powered diesel version of the Meteorite. At the end of the trials it was concluded that the original petrol engine offered the best all-round performance, with little to choose between the two diesels. Although, it was pointed out that the better slow-speed characteristics of the diesel gave it a slight edge on the FVRDE 'snake' test circuit.

This was not the only experiment with providing diesel power for the Mk 2 and in 1958/59, further trials were conducted, this time with a heavily-modified Mk 2

Antar which had been fitted with an AEC AVT1100 six-cylinder turbo-charged diesel engine producing 235bhp at 1800rpm from a capacity of 17,890cc. The power output was less than that offered by the Meteorite (260bhp), but the performance was impressive due to the more-favourable torque characteristics of the diesel. The Thornycroft company was

Below: FV12003 ballast tractor operated by the REME 'school' at Bordon.

The Glory Days of Heavy Haulage

eventually absorbed into the ACV Group in 1961, but this project was typical of areas of mutually-beneficial co-operation between the two companies before the merger.

In the end there was to be no diesel power for the Mk 2, but the trials provided valuable experience and the Rolls-Royce eight-cylinder C8SFL diesel was specified for the Mk 3, deliveries of which began in 1959.

In service
For their entire service lives, the Antars were almost exclusively deployed in Germany where they were assigned to BAOR, serving with Number 7 Tank Transporter Company RASC (7 TTC) with headquarters at Sennelager. Their role, in the event of war, would have been to move the armoured engineers and tank regiments from their bases in the BAOR sector, towards the border with East Germany and the Soviet Bloc where it was always believed the Soviet threat would turn to reality.

During the 'fifties and 'sixties, 7 TTC comprised four or five squadrons. Number 123 Squadron was based at Sennelager (later, I think, reformed as Number 3), Number 16 at Fallingbostel, and Numbers 612 and 617 MSO ('mixed service

organisation') based in Hamm and Fallingbostel, these latter two being staffed mainly by Poles and so-called 'white' Russians (Ukranians) who had elected to remain in Germany after the War (for various reasons!) and to serve with the British Army. As an example of the numbers of vehicles involved, Number 123 Squadron consisted of two troops, each holding 20 'trains' (a 'train' meaning an Antar and trailer), whilst Numbers 16 and 617 Squadrons each had three troops

of 20 Antar trains.

Fortunately, we never were actually at war with the Soviet Union, so the Antars spent most of their lives practising for war - hauling tanks from the docks in Antwerp to the barracks, and from the barracks to the training ranges at Sennelager, and to the NATO and British training areas at Bergen-Hohne and Soltau-Lüneburg.

Loading the tanks onto the trailers must have been a fine sight.

In the barracks it was done with 20 Antars abreast and the tanks were loaded one at a time from one end of the line. But in the field, the Regiment had developed a technique for loading 20 tanks simultaneously. The 20 tanks would be crewed-up and waiting with their

Left: Instrument panel of the Mk 2.

photograph: Mark Barnes >

Above: Front three-quarter view of the standard FV12002. Note the positions of the headlamps below the front bumper.

Technical specification

Nomenclature: tractor, 60 ton, GS, for semi-trailer, 6x4, FV12002; Thornycroft Antar Mk 2; tractor, 50 ton, GS, ballast body, 6x4, FV12003; Thornycroft Antar Mk 2.

Although these vehicles are now universally described as the 'Mk 2', at the time they were also occasionally referred to as either the 'Mk 1 for semi-trailer', or 'Mk 1B' (with ballast box).

Engine: Rover Meteorite Mk 204; eight cylinders in 60° 'V' formation; 18,012cc; overhead valves, two inlet and two exhaust per cylinder; dry sump; power output 260bhp at 2000rpm.
Transmission: 4F1Rx3; 6x4.
Suspension: live axles on semi-elliptical springs, inverted at rear.
Brakes: air pressure.
Construction: steel, ladder chassis; steel-framed and panelled cab; timber/steel composite ballast box on FV12003.
Electrical system: 24V.

Dimensions
Length, 332in; width, 111in; height, 120in.
Wheelbase, 186in; bogie centres, 62in.
Weight, FV12002, 43,186 lb; FV12003, 44,200 lb.

Above: Early Mk 2 Antars under construction - in this case the headlamps are placed above the bumper with guards mounted on the grille.

The Glory Days of Heavy Haulage

photograph: Mark Barnes

Mk 2 and Mk 3 Antars belonging to Rob Bailey.

nebulous that even the Director of Weapons Development (DWD) writing in a War Office memo in 1954 suggested that 'we should not interfere with the plot for increased production of Antars... if it (FV1205) is brought into service our orders for Antars could be cut down'. So confident were Thornycroft of their position as the sole supplier, that even as early as 1952 they were stating that 'no other tractor is under consideration for the same purpose'.

But the FV1205 went the way of most of the post-war specialised vehicles and the Antar remained the British Army's major tank-transporter tractor until the replacement of the Mk 3 and Mk 3A vehicles by the Scammell Commander in 1984.

photograph: Thornycroft Society

Left: Experimental Mk 2 fifth-wheel tractor fitted with the AEC AVT1100 turbocharged diesel engine. The bonnet has been heavily modified to accommodate the engine and resembles more closely the appearance of the subsequent Mk 3 Antars.

engines running. The Antars would drive forward one behind the other with a longish gap between each one and, as each tank transporter passed a predetermined point in the road (where the Squadron would have placed a 'load' sign), a tank would accelerate out, do a 90° turn, tuck in between two Antars and follow the transporter down the road. This process would continue until each of the 20 Antars was separated by a tank. The convoy would stop, the Antar crews would drop the ramps and all 20 tanks would load simultaneously. The transporter crews would lash down the load and they were ready to go. Apparently this could all be done within 30 minutes.

Typical loads would have included the Conqueror (exclusively on the 60-ton FV3001/FV3005 trailer), Centurion and Chieftain tanks, Centurion and Chieftain AVREs and bridgelayers, and the Abbott self-propelled gun; non-AFV loads would have covered bridge sections, boats and heavy machinery. The trailers intended for use with the Antar also included track guide positions for a number of Soviet and Eastern Bloc AFVs and these, too, might have formed the occasional load.

As the Mk 2 also became outdated, there was a period when Mk 2 Antars were serving alongside the more-powerful Mk 3 and this meant that in any mixed convoy the troop equipped with Mk 2 machines always had to run at the back since they were so slow!

During the early years of the Antar's

life, tank transporting in the UK was undertaken using Diamond Ts and was only supplemented by the use of Antars when the BAOR requirement was satisfied.

The future

By the end of the 'fifties, Thornycroft seemed to have been successful in ousting Scammell from their position of supplier of tank transporters to the British Army. Purchase of the Mk 2 Antar continued until 1957 when it was superseded in production by the FV12004/12006 Mk 3 and Mk 3A variant; in total some 353 vehicles were purchased against nine Ministry of Supply contracts.

Although in the 'background' there had always been a project for the Leyland-designed FV1205, so-called 'super heavy recovery tractor', this remained so

Further information

We would like to thank the Thornycroft Society, and particularly Chris Tree, for supplying some of the photographs which illustrate this article. If you are interested in joining the Society, contact the Membership Secretary Mervyn Annetts, at The New Coach House, Innersdown, Micheldever, Winchester, Hampshire SO21 3BW, (tel 01962 774574).

If you want to learn more about Thornycroft, look for copies of the following long out-of-print books:

Breakdown: A History Of Recovery Vehicles In The British Army.
Baxter, Brian S.
London, HMSO, 1989.
ISBN 0-11-290456-4.

Illustrated History Of Thornycroft Trucks And Buses.
Baldwin, Nick.
Sparkford, Haynes Publishing Group, 1989.
ISBN 0-85429-707-3.

Thanks also to the Bailey family for letting us climb all over their Antars

Antars aga

Pat Ware takes a look at the last of the breed – the FV12004/FV12006 Mk 3 Antar

WITHIN a few years of the end of WW2, the trusty, but arguably archaic, Scammell Pioneer TRMU30 tank transporters had been largely pensioned off, and the Diamond Ts were beginning to show serious signs of their age. Working with Leyland Motors, the Fighting Vehicles Research and Development Establishment (FVRDE) was developing all-new, purpose-designed 30- and 60-ton tank transporters as part of the FV1200 and FV1000 series. By the end of the decade there was no sign of the completion of either of these projects and, in 1951, purely as a stop-gap measure you understand, the Ministry of Supply purchased 15 Thornycroft Antar ballast tractors at a price of £8177 each.

Despite the use of a Diamond T style steel ballast body, and the removal of the civilian diesel engine in favour of a V8 Rover Meteorite petrol unit, the Mk 1 Antar – as it subsequently became known – was essentially a modification of the original oil-field tractor which had been developed by Thornycroft for civil engineers George Wimpey. Designated FV12001, the first example was delivered to FVRDE for trials on 27 June 1951.

The Antars entered service and the best part of another year passed with little real progress on the FV1200 and FV1000 projects. In April 1952, Thornycroft started work on building the first of 353 Mk 2 Antars. Initial production was of the

Standard FV12004 fifth-wheel tractor with the FV3011 semi-trailer leaving the REME 23 Base Workshop in Germany.

FV12002 fifth-wheel tractor – also known as the 'Mk 1 for semi-trailer' – but this was soon followed by the FV12003 wooden-bodied ballast tractor. The Mk 2 remained in production until about 1960 by which time the FV1000 and FV1200 projects had been virtually abandoned, and the ageing Diamond Ts had been up-engined. By now, the Antar was clearly the tank

transporter of choice but, unfortunately, it too was beginning to show its age, particularly on the German autobahns, where its lack of speed was becoming a hazard to other road users.

In early 1957, design work was started on what was to become the Antar Mk 3, and Thornycroft began to look seriously into ways of giving the machine a little more power.

The FV12006 ballast tractor used a similar wooden ballast box to the earlier Mk 2 vehicle; note the lifting rings on the corners of the box to allow it to be removed.

in...

Mixture of Mk 2 and Mk 3 Antars, probably photographed at the RASC Fallingbostel base in Germany. The date would have been the early 'sixties.

Technical specification

Nomenclature
- Tractor, 60 ton, GS, for semi trailer, 6x4, FV12004; Thornycroft Antar.
- Tractor, 50 ton, GS, for full trailer, 6x4, FV12006; Thornycroft Antar.

Engine: Rolls-Royce C8SFL-843; eight cylinders; 16,200cc; overhead valves; power output, 313bhp at 2,100rpm; torque, 934 lbf/ft at 1,500rpm.

Transmission: 6F1R; 6x4; manual inter-axle differential lock.
Suspension: live axles on semi-elliptical leaf springs.
Brakes: air pressure.
Construction: steel ladder chassis with steel-panelled cab.
Electrical system: 24V.

Dimensions
Length, 343in; width, 126in; height, 126in.
Wheelbase, 192in; bogie centres, 62in.
Weight, (FV12004) 51,568 lb, (FV12006) 48,221 lb.

It was no secret that the War Office would had always preferred that the Antar be diesel powered – as were the Diamond Ts - but for a long time no suitable home-grown power unit was available. When the Rolls-Royce 'C range' of diesel engines – from the old Sentinel works – was introduced in 1952, it seemed that perhaps this might be the way of the future. In 1956, a supercharged C6 was installed in a Mk 2 Antar and trialled head-to-head with a standard Meteorite-powered vehicle. In the event, it proved insufficiently powerful and the Antar had to wait until the eight-cylinder C8 version became available.

The use of the Rolls-Royce engine was probably a foregone conclusion, since it seemed to be the only available British engine of its type which offered sufficient power, but it was an expensive piece of kit, and in 1958/59 there was an experiment with an alternative power unit, perhaps with a view to reducing

expenditure. A standard Mk 2 Antar was fitted with a turbo-charged AEC AV1100 diesel engine and submitted to FVRDE for trials. The vehicle retained the standard Mk 2 cab, but was heavily modified around the bonnet, where it more-closely resembled the appearance of the Mk 3 machine. Although the vehicle acquitted itself well in trials, the Rolls-Royce C8 won the day and the AEC engine was not adopted. Nothing more came of this project and the trials vehicle was disposed of by FVRDE in 1971.

Back at Thornycroft's Basingstoke factory, work had begun on building three prototype Mk 3 Antars on 8 July 1957. The first of these machines to be constructed – chassis number 61183, registered RGX 981 – was actually delivered last, on 31 March 1958. Work on the remaining pair started in October, with Thornycroft's records showing that these vehicles (RGX 982 and RGX 983) were delivered in late February 1958, ahead of the first vehicle to be built.

Head-on view of the RAF Mk 3 Antar. This may have been some sort of prototype since it has one-piece windscreen glasses, and non-standard wing-mounted air cleaner.

Presumably all three vehicles were intended for reliability trials and at least one was submitted to FVRDE.

Production of the Mk 2 was resumed during the trials period.

Mechanically, the Mk 3 was streets ahead of the Mks 1 and 2. Alongside the

FV12006 ballast tractor coupled to the FV3601 50-ton drawbar trailer. ▶

Heavily-modified Mk 2 chassis fitted with the AEC AV1100 engine; note the not-unattractive combination of Mk 2 style cab and Mk 3 style nose.

Seen in side elevation, the bivouac-equipped ballast tractor is somewhat strangely-proportioned, apparently consisting of four separate 'lumps' which don't appear to have much connection – bonnet, cab, bivouac, ballast box.

new supercharged Rolls-Royce C8 engine – in this application, designated C8SFL – there was also a simplified six-speed transmission, replacing the old 4F1Rx3 system. Although, at 16,200cc, the capacity of the straight-eight C8SFL was actually slightly less than the old V8 Meteorite, the 333bhp gross power output was produced over a more usable band and, in combination with the new gearbox, both performance and economy were improved. Maximum speed was up to 40mph and fuel consumption was improved by almost 50%.

One criticism of the earlier Antars had been with the need to maintain high engine revolutions in order for the hydraulic power-assisted steering to work effectively and this often led to difficulties when manoeuvering in tight spaces. This problem was, at least,

partially solved by virtue of re-designed steering gear on the Mk 3.

However, despite the all-new engine and transmission, there was one area where the Mk 3 did not differ at all from its predecessors and that was in its propensity for overheating the axles. Continuous full power running always resulted in excessive oil temperature in the rear axles within a very short space of time. There were some experiments with the provision of an independent cooling system for the axle oil and, although this was not adopted, a re-designed axle was eventually produced which solved the problem.

The original Darlington winch used on

the Mk 1 and Mk 2 machines was replaced by a 20-ton Turner unit fitted behind the cab.

There was also a brand-new, all-steel cab. The wide, bluff radiator, broad bonnet and perpendicular, coach-built styling of the original were ousted in favour of a sleeker appearance. The bonnet was narrower at the nose which, of course, gave it a more pronounced taper, and the twin radiators were replaced by a single unit which was protected by a grille borrowed from the contemporary Big Ben truck. Big, box-shaped front wings, designed to accommodate the oil-bath air cleaners, replaced the old-fashioned rounded mudguards of the Mk 1 and Mk 2, and there were rear mudguards fitted irrespective of whether the vehicle was a fifth-wheel or ballast tractor. The flat windscreen of the original was replaced by a shallow 'V' shaped unit with opening bottom lights which provided the crew with a degree of control of conditions in the cab.

It was presumably still considered a bit 'cissy' to provide the crew with proper sleeping facilities and, although the new cab could accommodate a three-man crew in relative comfort, there was no bunk. The crews had to continue to rely on the somewhat make-shift 'bivouac' enclosure usually erected over the ballast box or the winch housing – a practice which had originated in WW2 when the crews used the big steel ballast box of the Diamond T tractors in this way. In a small gesture towards crew comfort, the lower parts of the windscreen were designed to open, and there were small opening vents fitted into the scuttle, low down on either side. But there was no heater or air-conditioning equipment, and despite the presence of these vents (and the opening windscreen) the cab became extremely hot in high ambient temperatures and

Tricky recovery operation of a Mk 3 Antar which has gone off the side of the German autobahn – note how a pair ballast tractors are being used as recovery vehicles.

▲ A classic rig – the FV12004 fifth-wheel tractor coupled to a well-loaded FV3011 50-ton semi-trailer.

REME Museum

eventually outward-facing scoops were fitted over the vents in an attempt to get more air into the interior.

The new cab was actually a standard Bonallack unit which had been widened by a foot or so by the insertion of a flat panel in the centre, and it was shared by other vehicles in the Thornycroft range as well as by the Guy Otter and Vixen. So, it would probably be picky to point out that the scuttle did not quite match the width of the bonnet, requiring a curious flat panel to be inserted to fill the gap on either side.

Nevertheless, the Mk 3 Antar was a very handsome and more modern-looking beast altogether.

Two more chassis were laid down in October 1958 and delivered in March 1959 but 'real' production did not get underway until April 1961. The FV12004 fifth-wheel tractor came first, followed by the FV12006

wooden-bodied ballast tractor – the latter being designated Mk 3A. In fact, the difference between the two machines was minimal, and it was a relatively-simple matter to convert the vehicle from one role to the other, and it was even suggested that all of the tractors were fitted with fifth-wheels and that the ballast body was simply fitted over the top when it was required.

In the early days, the fifth-wheel variant was often used with the Sankey FV3001 or FV3005 60-ton semi-trailers which had been produced for use with the Mk 2 variants, but latterly it was usually coupled to the sixteen-wheeled FV3011 50-ton semi-trailer. These trailers were constructed by Sankey, GKN and Taskers. By the time the Mk 3 Antar was entering service, the habit of using full trailers for tank transporting was falling from favour and the ballast tractors often ended up

This FV12004 Mk 3 was specially
prepared for the Thornycroft stand at
the 1963 Commercial Motor Show.

being used as recovery vehicles and
shunters. However, although photographs
showing this configuration are rare, the Mk
3A ballast tractor could also be used with
the Sankey or Dyson four-axle FV3601 50-
ton draw-bar trailer. There was also a so-
called 'dummy axle trailer' (FV3561) which
allowed an Antar to render assistance to a
second, disabled Antar, by means of a
suspended tow.

Production of the Mk 3 Antar continued
until 1966: the British Army took a total
210 examples, and total Antar production
was in the order of 730 units, with more
than 500 going overseas. Most of the Mk 3
Antars were based in Germany, where they
spent their time moving Chieftain and
Centurion main battle tanks from their
bases to the ranges at Höhne and Soltau. A
small number were operated by the RAF
for transporting aircraft fuselages.

Between them, the three 'marks' of Antar
clocked up 35 years service, with the Mk 3
covering 24 of those years – the last Antar
left Bulford Camp, Wiltshire on 30 January
1985 bound for British Car Auctions.
Ironically, the Antar was carried away on
the back of its replacement – the Scammell
Commander.

In 1968, both Thornycroft and Scammell
had been asked to investigate the
production of a new tank transporter,
which as far as Thornycroft was concerned,
meant a 'Mk 4 Antar'. However, by that
time the company had been sold to ACV,
and ACV, in turn had been sold to Leyland,
who also owned Scammell, which meant
that two parts of the Leyland empire were
competing for the same project. In 1970, in
a fit of rationalisation, the Thornycroft
factory at Basingstoke was closed and most
of the workforce moved to other parts of
the Leyland Group, with the 'heavy team'
going to Scammell's Watford plant. So, in
one of those ironic twists of fate, the

Commander was actually designed by
many of the same team that had produced
the Antar Mk 3 and it was effectively the
result of a marriage between the
Thornycroft Antar and the Scammell
Contractor, carrying both names at various
times during its early development!

But that, as they say in all the best books,
is another story..!

Little and large!